My Personal Prayer Book

for Mothers

Honor Books

07 06 05 04 03   10 9 8 7 6 5 4 3 2 1

My Personal Prayer Book for Mothers
ISBN 1-56292-754-X
Copyright © 2003 by Honor Books
An Imprint of Cook Communications Ministries
P.O. Box 55388
Tulsa, Oklahoma 74155

Manuscript preparation, as well as compilation and personalization of scriptures, by Betsy Williams, Tulsa, Oklahoma.

Presented to:

_____

From:

_____

Date:

_____

Contents

Introduction

What do you say to God when you don't know what to say? Sometimes during times of crisis, we know we have heard what God thinks about the things we need to ask Him for, but somehow in the stress of it all we are unable to bring His truths to mind. And sometimes we face events in our lives through which God is teaching us what we don't know—yet. So what do you pray when the words aren't there or you are not sure what you ought to be talking to Him about? *My Personal Prayer Book for Mothers* provides you with the keys to prayer by giving you very specific, very practical prayers on topics that women face as women and as mothers.

As an additional aid to your prayers, we have personalized each verse that precedes the prayer. God spoke His Word for you, and these scriptures on your concerns have personal pronouns to reflect His desire that you know His truth is for you. The wording of the *King James* has also been updated to the way you speak today so that you will experience, even more, the truth that God speaks to you today. As you can see by the example on the following page, the message God wants you to receive remains unchanged, but you are able to apply God's wonderful promise to yourself more easily with the personalized verse. And we have marked these verses plainly so you can tell the personalized verses at the beginning of the prayer from the verses on the preceding page which are not personalized.

Peace I leave with you, my peace I give unto you:
not as the world giveth, give I unto you. Let not
your heart be troubled, neither let it be afraid.
John 14:27 KJV

Peace You leave with me, Your peace You give to me;
You do not give as the world gives to me. I'm not to
let my heart be troubled, nor to let it be afraid.
John 14:27 PERSONALIZED

We have provided some scriptures on the page preceding the prayer to help you to find quickly what God says about your particular concern. In addition, for your everyday spiritual growth there is a section entitled "31 Days of Prayer" which contains a scripture and a very short prayer (we know mothers are very busy people), which covers the basics of the Christian life—such as the fruits of the Spirit, the Lord's Prayer, and many other helpful topics. As you are praying you will also find some pages at the back useful for entering your own personal prayer requests, and also some pages for you to enter the answers. When you use this book, you will be able to say with delight as a woman and mother, "This is *My Personal Prayer Book!*"

Abandonment

Those who know Your name will put their trust in You;
For You, LORD, have not forsaken those who seek You.
Psalm 9:10 NKJV

The LORD loves justice,
And does not forsake His godly ones;
They are preserved forever.
Psalm 37:28 NASB

The Lord will not abandon his chosen people,
for that would dishonor his great name. He made you
a special nation for himself—just because he wanted to!
1 Samuel 12:22 TLB

I will be with you as I was with Moses.
I will not fail you or abandon you.
Joshua 1:5 NLT

When my father and my mother forsake me,
then You, LORD, will take me up.
Psalm 27:10 PERSONALIZED

COMFORTING FATHER,

I may not have been abandoned as an infant on a
stranger's front porch, yet this feeling has engulfed my soul.
As human beings, we long for intimacy with each other
and to trust one another. I believe this was Your plan all
along, yet I have been forsaken by some of the people I
have loved most.

In Your Scripture, You remind me of Your own precious
Son who experienced these same feelings of abandonment
when on the cross He cried out, "My God, My God, why
hast Thou forsaken Me?" He knows my pain for He has
trodden this path before me.

I am thankful for such a gracious Savior who said He
would never leave me nor forsake me. I am comforted and
reassured, knowing my feelings of grief can be washed away
by Your love, Your holy presence. Thank You for Your
faithfulness to me, for abiding with me till the end.

AMEN.

Abuse

He delivers me from my enemies.
You also lift me up above those who rise against me;
You have delivered me from the violent man.
Psalm 18:48 NKJV

O LORD, I have come to you for protection . . .
Bend down and listen to me;
Rescue me quickly.
Be for me a great rock of safety,
a fortress where my enemies cannot reach me.
You are my rock and my fortress.
For the honor of your name, lead me out of this peril.
Psalm 31:1-3

Bring to an end the violence of the wicked
and make the righteous secure.
My shield is God Most High.
Psalm 7:9-10 NIV

On the day I call for help, my enemies will be defeated.
I know that God is on my side.
Psalm 56:9 NCV

*You sent from above, You took me. . . . You delivered me
from my strong enemy, and from those who hated me: for
they were too strong for me. . . . You brought me forth also into
a large place; You delivered me, because You delighted in me.*
Psalm 18:16-17,19 PERSONALIZED

FATHER OF MERCIES,

Abuse is something that happens to other people, I
thought, not to me. Yet, here I am, feeling trapped and unable
to escape. At first I thought it was an accident, and he assured
me it was. I was able to forgive, confident that it wouldn't
happen again. I kept thinking it was my fault, that maybe
there was something inherently wrong with me that deserved
this harsh treatment. But Your Word tells me that isn't true.

Words and actions have bruised me, body and soul, each
instance sending me on a deeper and deeper spiral down-
ward. Now I feel I have nothing left. But You give hope.

You come to me as a gentle Shepherd, loving me, reassuring me. Dear Lord, help me find the way of escape. Come
rescue me! Shine Your light in my darkness, so I may find
the way to the life of freedom You promise Your children.
Thank You for hearing me when I call.

AMEN.

Acceptance

Christ accepted you, so you should accept each other.
This will bring glory to God.
Romans 15:7 NCV

He has been merciful . . . by remembering his
sacred promise . . . making us holy and acceptable,
ready to stand in his presence forever.
Luke 1:72-73,75 TLB

You love me! You are holding my right hand!
Psalm 73:23 TLB

God will accept us in the same way he accepted
Abraham—when we believe the promises of God
who brought back Jesus our Lord from the dead.
Romans 4:24 TLB

Having predestined me to being adopted as Your child by Jesus Christ to Yourself, according to the good pleasure of Your will, to the praise of the glory of Your grace, whereby You have made me accepted in Your beloved son.
Ephesians 1:5-6 PERSONALIZED

LOVING FATHER,

Why is it that sometimes, in spite of all my best efforts, I never quite feel like I belong? My life is not so different from most mothers, or even other people. Yet even though I do many of the same things others do, I often feel out of step.

Many follow the crowd, going with the latest trends and attitudes, but this is not the life to which You have called me. You urge me to come out from among the world and to be separate, to be in the world but not of it.

No matter who rejects me, whether I feel like I fit in or not, I can rest in Your promise that You chose me and You have adopted me into Your family. No matter what, I am accepted by You, according to the good pleasure of Your will. Thank You for making me Your child. I'm glad that I belong to You.

AMEN.

Addiction
Help for Me

Throw off your old evil nature . . . . Yes, you must
be a new and different person, holy and good.
Clothe yourself with this new nature.
Ephesians 4:22,24 TLB

Blessed be the Lord, the God of Israel;
he came and set his people free.
Luke 1:68 THE MESSAGE

"If therefore the Son shall make you free, you shall be free indeed."
John 8:36 NASB

Stand fast therefore in the liberty by which Christ has made us free,
and do not be entangled again with a yoke of bondage.
Galatians 5:1 NKJV

Sin shall not have dominion over me:
for I am not under the law, but under grace.
Romans 6:14 PERSONALIZED

ALL-POWERFUL FATHER,

Nothing is too difficult for You, but many things are too difficult for me. I feel like I have come to the end of myself and that I cannot break free. I was determined not to become addicted. I thought I was stronger, that I would be the exception. I would indulge just enough to enjoy myself and unwind, but now I find I cannot stop.

Now I know that it takes Your power to break out of addiction's bondage. You conquered sin when You rose from the dead, and You gave me that victory as a gift. I repent of my pride for thinking I could do this by myself, and I humbly request Your help. From now on I will rest in the strength You give. Thank You for Your grace to deliver me and for making me more than a conqueror through Christ.

AMEN.

Addiction
Help for My Child

"I will give you the keys of the kingdom of heaven;
whatever you bind on earth will be bound in heaven,
and whatever you loose on earth will be loosed in heaven."
Matthew 16:19 NIV

The LORD gives freedom to the prisoners.
The LORD opens the eyes of the blind;
The LORD raises those who are bowed down.
Psalm 146:7-8 NKJV

He has rescued us from the one who rules
in the kingdom of darkness, and he has brought us
into the Kingdom of his dear Son. God has purchased
our freedom with his blood and has forgiven all our sins.
Colossians 1:13-14 NLT

The law of the Spirit of life in Christ Jesus has
set you free from the law of sin and of death.
Romans 8:2 NRSV

The weapons of my warfare are not carnal, but mighty
through You, God, to the pulling down of strongholds.
2 Corinthians 10:4 PERSONALIZED

FATHER IN HEAVEN,

Your promises assure me that You are an ever-present help in time of need, so I come to You on behalf of my child. Having been taken captive by the rulers of darkness, he is caught in the web of addiction and cannot find his way out.

It has wreaked havoc in my soul as I have stood by, feeling helpless to do anything. Memories of happy days gone by have been replaced by cold realities of today.

However, You remind me that I am not helpless. The weapons You have given me are not of this earth, but they are mighty through You to pull down the strongholds of the evil one. Help me to stand firm when it seems nothing is changing and to trust that You are at work. I take comfort in Your promise to always hear my prayer, and I thank You that I can trust You with my child's life.

AMEN.

Aging

I, Wisdom, will make the hours of your day more
profitable and the years of your life more fruitful.
Proverbs 9:11 TLB

I will be your God through all your lifetime,
yes, even when your hair is white with age. I made
you and I will care for you. I will carry you along.
Isaiah 46:4 TLB

The silver-haired head is a crown of glory,
If it is found in the way of righteousness.
Proverbs 16:31 NKJV

Store my commands in your heart, for they
will give you a long and satisfying life.
Proverbs 3:1-2 NLT

*With me, the aged, is wisdom; and in
the length of my days, understanding.*
Job 12:12 PERSONALIZED

EVERLASTING FATHER,

I've heard it said that the golden years are often tarnished, but I know this is not Your plan. Your Word offers a better way, one I desire: "As your days, *so shall* your strength *be*" (Deuteronomy 33:25 NKJV). May I be like Moses and die at a ripe old age, with eyes that are not dim and vigor that is not diminished.

Lord, I want to make my life count. I want to become one of the older women You use to teach the younger women to live godly lives and to love their husbands and children. Use my years of experience and wisdom for good.

You have promised to satisfy me with a long life, and although my body ages, my inner self, soul and spirit, grows younger day by day. Continue to strengthen me with power inwardly, and bless my days with health. May I glorify You all of my days.

AMEN.

Anger

One who is slow to anger is better than the mighty,
and one whose temper is controlled than one who captures a city.
Proverbs 16:32 NRSV

Everyone must be quick to hear, slow to speak and slow to anger;
for the anger of man does not achieve the righteousness of God.
James 1:19-20 NASB

A hot-tempered man stirs up dissension,
but a patient man calms a quarrel.
Proverbs 15:18 NIV

Those with good sense are slow to anger,
and it is their glory to overlook an offense.
Proverbs 19:11 NRSV

*I am to be angry, and not to sin; I'm not to let the sun
go down upon my anger nor give place to the devil.*
Ephesians 4:26-27 PERSONALIZED

LOVING FATHER,

I think the emotion of anger is the most misunderstood of all emotions. I know I am to love my neighbor, but I have thought being angry was taboo. Not wanting to displease You, I have denied my wrath by internalizing it, hoping it would go away. Nonetheless, my anger has only festered below the surface, eating at my soul.

Thankfully, Your Word reveals a more balanced solution. Although human wrath doesn't work Your righteousness, getting angry is a fact of life. What I do with that anger seems to be the key. Help me to find constructive ways to diffuse my anger, to be angry but not let it drive me to sin. Help me to recognize the trigger points and find ways to communicate my pain without hurting others. I ask You to bathe my raw emotions in Your love and to restore me to that place of peace.

AMEN.

Anxiety

An anxious heart weighs a man down,
but a kind word cheers him up.
Proverbs 12:25 NIV

"Don't be anxious about tomorrow. God will take
care of your tomorrow too. Live one day at a time."
Matthew 6:34 TLB

The Holy Spirit has been at work in your hearts,
cleansing you with the blood of Jesus Christ and making
you to please him. May God bless you richly and grant
you increasing freedom from all anxiety and fear.
1 Peter 1:2 TLB

Blessed are those who trust in the LORD,
whose trust is the LORD.
They shall be like a tree planted by water . . .
in the year of drought it is not anxious,
and it does not cease to bear fruit.
Jeremiah 17:7-8 NRSV

*Peace You leave with me, Your peace You give to me;
You do not give as the world gives to me. I'm not
to let my heart be troubled, nor to let it be afraid.*
John 14:27 PERSONALIZED

GOD OF PEACE,

As I go through my day, I find myself getting more tense
with each passing hour. Oftentimes I become agitated and
irritable with those around me, and it affects the atmosphere of our home. There are so many things going on in
my own life right now, things over which I have no control,
and I find myself getting anxious. My anxiety deepens to
fear when I think of the world my children will face after I
am gone.

Help me to follow Jesus' example of walking in peace.
How wonderful it was that even during a fierce storm, He
was found napping, confident You were watching over the
ones He loved.

Jesus promised me His peace, so I choose to receive that
peace today. Help me to stop allowing myself to become
agitated. Help me instead to meditate on Your promises to
watch over my family and me.

AMEN.

Assurance

God is not a man, that He should lie,
Nor a son of man, that He should repent;
Has He said, and will He not do it?
Or has He spoken, and will He not make it good?
Numbers 23:19 NASB

I know whom I have believed, and am convinced that he is
able to guard what I have entrusted to him for that day.
2 Timothy 1:12 NIV

"I give them eternal life, and they will never perish.
No one will snatch them out of my hand.
What my Father has given me is greater than all else,
and no one can snatch it out of the Father's hand."
John 10:28-29 NRSV

He has appointed a day on which He will judge the world in
righteousness by the Man whom He has ordained. He has
given assurance of this to all by raising Him from the dead.
Acts 17:31 NKJV

I am persuaded, that neither death, nor life, . . .
nor things present, nor things to come, . . . nor any
other creature, shall be able to separate me from the
love of God, which is in Christ Jesus my Lord.
Romans 8:38-39 PERSONALIZED

FATHER GOD,

In this world, there are not many assurances, not many things or people I can count on. Contracts are not binding and one's word is rarely her bond. Life in this world is like shifting sand, unstable and ever changing.

But that is not the case with You, blessed Father. I appreciate that You always keep Your promises and that You never change. You are the one true Rock on which I can build my life. Regardless of the storms of life that come my way and try to knock me off my foundation, I am encouraged that I can count on You. It is a great comfort to know that nothing, absolutely nothing, can separate me from Your love. "Blessed assurance, Jesus is mine. O what a foretaste of glory Divine." Sometimes the old hymns say it best, and lyrics like these are ones I want to meditate on.

AMEN.

Attitude

The mind set on the flesh is death, but
the mind set on the Spirit is life and peace.
Romans 8:6 NASB

All of you be of one mind, having compassion for one another; love
as brothers, be tenderhearted, be courteous; not returning evil for
evil or reviling for reviling, but on the contrary blessing, knowing
that you were called to this, that you may inherit a blessing.
1 Peter 3:8-9 NKJV

May God who gives patience, steadiness, and encouragement
help you to live in complete harmony with each other—
each with the attitude of Christ toward the other.
Romans 15:5 TLB

Your attitude should be the kind that
was shown us by Jesus Christ.
Philippians 2:5 TLB

I'm to be renewed in the spirit of my mind;
And I'm to put on my new nature, which in Your
likeness is created in righteousness and true holiness.
Ephesians 4:23-24 PERSONALIZED

HEAVENLY FATHER,

In Your Word, You talk a great deal about our thoughts and attitudes. To be sure, this is an area in which I could use some help. Like many things in life, a bad attitude can become a habit, and I feel it's time to make a change.

I know it's up to me to set the tone for our family, and my attitude plays a major part. Please forgive me for allowing myself to give in to seeing things in a negative light. Your Word says I have the mind of Christ, and I want to think His thoughts. Help me to recognize when a bad attitude tries to creep in. Help me to rest my eyes on You and to trust You to work everything out for my good. Help me to see the good in every person I meet, the good in every situation I face. Let my attitude be one so filled with Your thoughts that I become a beacon of light to those around me.

AMEN.

Beauty

Charm is deceitful and beauty is vain,
But a woman who fears the LORD, she shall be praised.
Proverbs 31:30 NASB

God does not see the same way people see. People look at
the outside of a person, but the LORD looks at the heart.
1 Samuel 16:7 NCV

The LORD takes pleasure in His people;
He will beautify the humble with salvation.
Psalm 149:4 NKJV

He has made everything beautiful in its time.
Ecclesiastes 3:11 NIV

I am not to let my adorning be outward adorning of braiding my hair, and of wearing gold jewelry, or putting on fine clothes; but I am to let it be the hidden person of the heart, that which does not decay. Let my beauty come from a meek and quiet spirit, which is in the sight of God of great value.
1 Peter 3:3-4 PERSONALIZED

HEAVENLY FATHER,

It is my sincere desire to be beautiful in Your eyes, according to the standard You have set. Your Word explains that You are more interested in what goes on within my heart than how I adorn myself on the outside. Jesus rebuked the Pharisees for being like whitewashed mausoleums, which appear beautiful on the outside but are filled with dead men's bones. Similarly, many women appear lovely at first glance, yet if they possess sour attitudes, their beauty is tainted. In contrast, there are rather ordinary-looking women who radiate Your life and joy.

Father, help me to value what You value and to incorporate those attributes into my life. Regardless of the personality You have given me, I desire to develop that gentle and quiet spirit, which You prize. May the fruit of Your Spirit flow through me continually, beautifying my spirit in You.

AMEN.

Blessings

*Praise be to the God and Father of our LORD Jesus Christ. In
Christ, God has given us every spiritual blessing in heaven.*
Ephesians 1:3 NCV

*You, O LORD, will bless the righteous;
With favor You will surround him as with a shield.*
Psalm 5:12 NKJV

*Salvation belongs to the LORD.
Your blessing is upon Your people.*
Psalm 3:8 NKJV

*The blessing of the LORD brings wealth,
and he adds no trouble to it.*
Proverbs 10:22 NIV

You will make my people and the places round about my hill a blessing; and You will cause the shower to come down in its season; there shall be, for me, showers of blessing.
Ezekiel 34:26 Personalized

Blessed Father,

What a marvelous plan You have for Your children—and I am thankful to be one of them. Your nature flowing through me makes me eager to be a blessing to the people in my world, fulfilling Your design for my life.

If I will abide in Your Word and adhere to Your will, You assure me that You will bless my comings and goings, making me the head and not the tail. Like a gentle spring rain watering the earth, showers of blessing will nourish my soul. I bless You, O Lord, and as You instruct, I will not forget that You forgave my sins and healed my diseases. You generously fill my life with good things so that my youth is renewed like the eagle's. And You cause goodness and mercy to follow me all the days of my life, enabling me to be a vessel of that blessing to others.

May my life bring glory to You.

Amen.

Burdens

"My yoke is easy and my burden is light."
Matthew 11:30 NIV

Bear one another's burdens,
and thereby fulfill the law of Christ.
Galatians 6:2 NASB

Now I will relieve your shoulder of its burden;
I will free your hands from their heavy tasks.
Psalm 81:6 NLT

The LORD *lifts the burdens of those bent beneath their loads.*
The LORD *loves the righteous.*
Psalm 146:8 NLT

I am to cast my burden upon You, LORD, and You shall sustain me: You will never allow the righteous to be moved.
Psalm 55:22 PERSONALIZED

CARING FATHER,

It is a relief to know that You want me to give my burdens to You. Life has presented me with heavy circumstances, which even now threaten to weigh me down. Wanting to help those I love, I have attempted to shoulder their problems as well. Each additional burden has caused me to sink lower and lower, oppressing me with the weight of it all. Now I need help.

I remember Your Word and light begins to dawn. You remind me that Jesus said His yoke is easy, that His burden would be light. I was not created to be a burden bearer; for You alone, God Almighty, can carry the load. So the next time I am tempted to give extra baggage a ride and to handle my troubles all by myself, remind me, dear Father, to pass them to You, knowing You can carry them all.

AMEN.

Burnout

Those who wait for the LORD
Will gain new strength;
They will mount up with wings like eagles,
They will run and not get tired,
They will walk and not become weary.
Isaiah 40:31 NASB

You have made me as strong as a wild bull.
How refreshed I am by your blessings!
Psalm 92:10 TLB

Never forget your promises to me your servant,
for they are my only hope. They give me strength in
all my troubles; how they refresh and revive me!
Psalm 119:49 TLB

By a miracle God sent them food to eat and water to drink there
in the desert; they drank the water that Christ gave them. He
was there with them as a mighty Rock of spiritual refreshment.
1 Corinthians 10:3 TLB

You make me lie down in green pastures;
You lead me beside the still waters.
You restore my soul.
Psalm 23:2-3 PERSONALIZED

HEAVENLY FATHER,

Life has been coming at me so hard and fast that I feel like I've been scrambling on the treadmill of life, always in motion but not making much progress. Perhaps I've become fatigued by refusing to stop and rest. But how do I rest when parenting is such a full-time job, filling twenty-four hours a day? No matter how fast I run, there is always another floor to be swept, a dispute to referee, or a meal to be prepared.

Your Word calls me to join *You* for a while. Green pastures and still waters are the images You paint, providing repose for my weary mind.

Father, forgive me for taking so long to stop. Instead of sprinting through this busy life, help me to slow down and take it at the pace You have designed for me. Restore my soul to wholeness to walk with You again.

AMEN.

Comfort

Even though I walk through the darkest valley,
I fear no evil;
for you are with me;
your rod and your staff—they comfort me.
Psalm 23:4 NRSV

I will not leave you comfortless: I will come to you.
John 14:18

As a mother comforts her child,
so will I comfort you;
and you will be comforted.
Isaiah 66:13 NIV

"The Comforter, which is the Holy Ghost, whom the Father will
send in my name, he shall teach you all things, and bring all
things to your remembrance, whatsoever I have said unto you."
John 14:26 KJV

You, Lord, will increase my greatness,
and comfort me on every side.
Psalm 71:21 PERSONALIZED

LOVING FATHER,

You must have known that we would need a great deal of comfort during our stay here on Earth. When Jesus was about to return to You, He said it was necessary for Him to go, so He could send the Comforter to sustain us in this life.

The word *comforter* conjures up a pleasant image in my soul. Cozily wrapped up on all sides by Your Spirit, I am merely an observer as the storms of life rage around me, unable to touch me. I need only sit and watch as Your Spirit gives me all I need while my enemies see my good fortune and wonder. I am never without comfort, for I dwell in Your Holy Spirit, my refuge. Ever waiting to succor me, Father, You surround me on all sides.

So often I thank You, Father, and I glorify Your Son. Today I remember the gift of Your Spirit and thank You for the comfort You provide.

AMEN.

Commitment

Let us not lose heart in doing good, for in due time
we will reap if we do not grow weary.
Galatians 6:9 NASB

Be strong and do not give up, for your work will be rewarded.
2 Chronicles 15:7 NIV

Jesus said, "Throw your lot in with the One that God has sent.
That kind of a commitment gets you in on God's works."
John 6:29 THE MESSAGE

Let's keep focused on that goal, those of us who want
everything God has for us. If any of you have something
else in mind, something less than total commitment,
God will clear your blurred vision—you'll see it yet!
Now that we're on the right track, let's stay on it.
Philippians 3:15-16 THE MESSAGE

"Behold, I am coming quickly! Hold fast what
you have, that no one may take your crown."
Revelation 3:11 NKJV

> LORD, *who shall abide in Your temple? . . . I will, if*
> *I walk uprightly, work righteousness, and speak the truth*
> *in my heart. If in my eyes a wicked person is condemned;*
> *but I honor those who fear You,* LORD. *I will if I keep*
> *my promises to my own cost and refuse to default.*
> Psalm 15:1-2,4 PERSONALIZED

DEAR FATHER,

No matter how much I want to serve You and to be faithful, there are times I struggle with commitment, even though my heart wants to press on. I believe Jesus said it best when He said that the spirit is willing, but the human nature without You is weak. In the past, I've let You and others down, and I need Your forgiveness.

Cleanse me from my failings; strengthen my resolve to be a committed follower of Jesus, a disciple You can count on.

I long to dwell in Your temple and to worship in Your courts, O God. Help me to obey You in all things and to avoid any action or motive that would hinder my entrance into Your presence. As situations spring up along my path, I rely on you to make me a person who does what is right and loving no matter what the cost.

AMEN.

Condemnation

Now there is no condemnation for those who belong to Christ Jesus.
Romans 8:1 NLT

The Lord blesses good men and condemns the wicked.
Proverbs 12:2 TLB

Who then will condemn us? Will Christ Jesus?
No, for he is the one who died for us and
was raised to life for us and is sitting at the place
of highest honor next to God, pleading for us.
Romans 8:34 NLT

It is wrong for a judge to favor the
wicked and condemn the innocent.
Proverbs 18:5 TLB

*You did not send Your Son into the world to
condemn the world (including me); but that I
and the world might be saved through Him.*
John 3:17 PERSONALIZED

LOVING FATHER,

What a revolutionary thought it is to realize that You do
not condemn me. False religion paints a deceitful portrait
of You as a tyrannical despot seeking to oppress Your sub-
jects, but the opposite is true. You did not send Jesus to
condemn me but to save me and give me abundant life. It is
Your enemy who seeks to destroy my life, using condemnation clothed in religious garb to do his undercover work.
Help me not to be fooled by his lies.

Now that Jesus has become my sacrifice, I am no longer
condemned because Jesus bore it all. Instead of seeking to
oppress me, He has come to set me free.

Glorious liberty can refresh my soul when I finally
understand the burden has been lifted. Let Your love flow
throughout my being, washing away all the stain of disap-
proval and filling me with joy.

AMEN.

Conflict
In the Home

Starting a quarrel is like a leak in a dam.
So stop the quarrel before a fight breaks out.
Proverbs 17:14 NCV

BEHOLD, how good and how pleasant it is
For brothers to dwell together in unity! . . .
It is like the dew of Hermon,
Coming down upon the mountains of Zion;
For there the LORD commanded the blessing—
life forever.
Psalm 133:1,3 NASB

I appeal to you . . . in the name of our Lord Jesus Christ,
that all of you agree with one another so that
there may be no divisions among you and that
you may be perfectly united in mind and thought.
1 Corinthians 1:10 NIV

Put away from you all bitterness and wrath and anger and
wrangling and slander, together with all malice, and be
kind to one another, tenderhearted, forgiving one another,
as God in Christ has forgiven you.
Ephesians 4:31-32 NRSV

You will give us one heart, and one way, that I may reverence
You forever, for my good, and my children's after me.
Jeremiah 32:39 PERSONALIZED

HEAVENLY FATHER,

Conflict is something I have a difficult time living with, yet it has crept into our home. Hurtful words and disagreeable attitudes have bruised tender emotions and threaten to divide us from within. Instead of a place of refuge, our dwelling has become a battle zone.

But it does not have to stay this way, and I seek Your assistance, holy Father. I ask You to forgive each family member, including me, for allowing strife to enter our family. Thank You for forgiving us and showing us the way a Godly family is to operate. Instead of dysfunction, reveal healthy ways for us to relate.

You promise to give us one heart and one way, that we might reverence You forever, for our good and for our children after us. Help us to resolve our differences, and restore us to a place of unity, so we may leave a Godly heritage for generations to come.

AMEN.

Conflict
Outside the Home

Do not be overcome by evil, but overcome evil with good.
Romans 12:21 NRSV

You shall not hate your fellow countryman in your heart . . .
but you shall love your neighbor as yourself; I am the LORD.
Leviticus 19:17-18 NASB

Hatred stirs up strife,
But love covers all sins.
Proverbs 10:12 NKJV

Avoid foolish and ignorant disputes,
knowing that they generate strife.
2 Timothy 2:23 NKJV

Where envying and strife is in me,
there is confusion and every evil work.
James 3:16 PERSONALIZED

FATHER GOD,

It must disappoint You when You see strife. As one of Your children, I do not reflect the life of Jesus when I fall for this trap of the enemy of my soul. Issues, so important to me at the time, are usually insignificant when viewed from Your perspective.

And I find upon examination that a jealous or a bitter, unforgiving attitude makes me prone to doing the wrong thing in these relationships. Please forgive me and cleanse me. Give me Your heart of love for those who oppose me. You've instructed me to do whatever I can to cultivate peace, so that is the path I choose to walk.

The Scripture states that the world will know I am Jesus' disciple when I love others. What a great opportunity this provides to demonstrate my faith. I repent of everything I have done to contribute to the deterioration of this relationship, and I ask You to allow Your love through me to bring healing to this breach.

AMEN.

Contentment

Better is a little that the righteous person has
than the abundance of many wicked.
For the arms of the wicked shall be broken,
but the LORD upholds the righteous.
Psalm 37:16-17 NRSV

Better a handful with quietness
Than both hands full, together with toil and grasping for the wind.
Ecclesiastes 4:6 NKJV

Better is a little with the fear of the LORD
than great treasure and trouble therewith.
Proverbs 15:16

Keep your lives free from the love of money and be
content with what you have, because God has said,
"Never will I leave you; never will I forsake you."
Hebrews 13:5 NIV

I have learned, in whatever state of affairs
I find myself, therewith to be content.
Philippians 4:11 PERSONALIZED

PEACEFUL FATHER,

I find myself telling my children on a regular basis to be content with what they have. Forever asking me for something new, it seems what they have is never enough. Yet I'm not much better off when I look at my own heart. Keenly aware of what others have, I begin to take inventory of the things that I now lack. Instead of being thankful for the many blessings You've given me, instead I yearn for more.

Since the apostle Paul learned to be content in spite of all the difficulties he faced, there is hope for me that I can do the same. His life encourages me that godliness with contentment is a lifestyle worthy of pursuit.

Father, I repent of my discontent and for not being more grateful for my many blessings. The next time I begin to complain about what I don't have, I ask You to gently remind me to choose contentment once again.

AMEN.

Courage

Be strong, and let your heart take courage,
all you who wait for the LORD.
Psalm 31:24 NRSV

THE LORD is my light and my salvation;
Whom shall I fear?
The LORD is the strength of my life;
Of whom shall I be afraid?
Psalm 27:1 NKJV

Be strong and of good courage, do not fear nor be
afraid of them; for the LORD your God, He is the One
who goes with you. He will not leave you nor forsake you.
Deuteronomy 31:6 NKJV

The LORD is my strength and my shield;
my heart trusts in him, and I am helped.
My heart leaps for joy
and I will give thanks to him in song.
Psalm 28:7 NIV

Have You not commanded me? I am to be strong and of good courage; I am not to be afraid, neither am I to be dismayed: for the LORD my God is with me wherever I go.
Joshua 1:9 PERSONALIZED

ALMIGHTY GOD,

I feel like the cowardly lion, lacking the fortitude to face life with a brave heart. I know this is common, but reading in the Bible about Joshua, I find hope. I may not face huge armies as he did, but the situations I face seem just as frightening to me.

If I remember You promised that You are always with me, my courage begins to grow. Your promise that we will be together wherever the road may lead helps me to see my giants with a fresh perspective. Like Joshua and others, I look to You, knowing My help comes from You, Lord, the Maker of heaven and earth. You will never leave me defenseless as I carry out Your will in my family and my life.

You may choose not to eliminate all my problems, but with You I can face anything, confident that You control the outcome.

AMEN.

Deliverance

*You deliver the humble but condemn
the proud and haughty ones.*
Psalm 18:27 TLB

*The Lord will always deliver me from all evil
and will bring me into his heavenly kingdom.*
2 Timothy 4:18 TLB

*God-strengthened, we're delivered from evil—
when we run to him, he saves us.*
Psalm 37:40 THE MESSAGE

*Now, the Lord is the Spirit, and wherever
the Spirit of the Lord is, he gives freedom.*
2 Corinthians 3:17 NLT

You are my hiding place; You will preserve me from trouble;
You will encompass me with songs of deliverance.
Psalm 32:7 PERSONALIZED

ALMIGHTY FATHER,

I can get myself into some terrible situations, which seem to have no way of escape. Sometimes it is because of my own choices that I run into a dead end. Other times I fall victim to life's circumstances, unable to see a way through.

But You never leave me without hope, and You provide a hiding place for me. You deliver me from harm and fill my life with songs about Your faithfulness.

Though my enemies pursue me like the Egyptians pursued the children of Israel toward the Red Sea, I go forward with growing confidence as I hide myself in You. And just when I think there's no place left to run, You part the sea before me and I cross over on dry ground. My enemies are swallowed up, never to hinder me again.

I praise You ahead of time for my deliverance, Father. I know I can rely on You.

AMEN.

Depression
Resulting from a Chemical Imbalance

God anointed Jesus of Nazareth with the Holy Spirit and
with power. Then Jesus went around doing good and healing
all who were oppressed by the Devil, for God was with him.
Acts 10:38 NLT

O LORD my God, I cried out to You,
And You healed me.
O LORD, You brought my soul up from the grave;
You have kept me alive, that I should not go down to the pit.
Psalm 30:2-3 NKJV

He spoke the word that healed you,
that pulled you back from the brink of death.
Psalm 107:20 THE MESSAGE

"I will restore you to health
and heal your wounds," declares the LORD.
Jeremiah 30:17 NIV

Hear me quickly, O LORD: my spirit fails. Don't hide Your face from me, or I will be like those who die. Make me able to perceive Your lovingkindness in the morning; for I trust in You. Cause me to know the way I should walk; for I lift up my soul to You.
Psalm 143:7-8 PERSONALIZED

HEAVENLY FATHER,

Like David of old, I pour out my heart to You and cry to You for help. Caught in the quagmire, I seem unable to move, helpless to lift myself up to see the light. Had I not believed that I would experience Your kindness here and now, I would have despaired totally and sunk into the depths. Darkness surrounds me, continually pulling me down, further and further till I think I can't hold on. The ground becomes slippery as I continue to slide.

But Your Word offers me hope to be delivered from this dreadful curse. I praise You now, God my Savior, for hearing my call. I know You will answer my cries to You with the strength of Your right hand, reaching out to me and pulling me up to safety.

Pour in the balm of Gilead to soothe my fractured nerves and restore my sense of well-being. Give me wisdom to know the steps I can take to assist in my recovery.

AMEN.

Depression
Resulting from Hopelessness

*Why be discouraged and sad? Hope in God! For I know
that I shall again have plenty of reason to praise him
for all that he will do. He is my help! He is my God!*
Psalm 42:5,11 TLB

*He will not break the bruised reed, nor quench the dimly burning
flame. He will encourage the fainthearted, those tempted to despair.*
Isaiah 42:3 TLB

*Truly the eye of the LORD is on those who fear him,
on those who hope in his steadfast love,
to deliver their soul from death,
and to keep them alive in famine.*
Psalm 33:18-19 NRSV

*The LORD himself will lead you and be with you.
He will not fail you or abandon you,
so do not lose courage or be afraid.*
Deuteronomy 31:8 TEV

Many say of my soul, "There is no help for her in God."
But You, O LORD, are a shield for me; my glory,
and the One who lifts my head.
Psalm 3:2-3 PERSONALIZED

GOD OF HOPE,

Once again I find myself at the end of my rope, exhausted, my hopes dashed against the rocks. Satan has desired to crush me as wheat, but he will not succeed; for Jesus, I know, is praying to You for me. When the whole world mocks that there is no hope, You speak up and declare You are turning things around.

Against all hope, You give me fresh living hope, promising to win the victory for me. You will lift my head high with confidence and remind me of Your faithfulness, breathing life into my weary soul once again.

I set my mind on You and what You care about, filling my thoughts with those things that are good, true, and valued by all. I remind myself of the past conquests You've made against all odds, and I am heartened You will do the same for me. I bless you, my Father, for being my hope.

AMEN.

Destiny

Each person is given something to do that shows who God is.
1 Corinthians 12:7 THE MESSAGE

*We are His workmanship, created in Christ Jesus
for good works, which God prepared beforehand,
that we would walk in them.*
Ephesians 2:10 NASB

*Call to Me, and I will answer you, and show you
great and mighty things, which you do not know.*
Jeremiah 33:3 NKJV

*"No eye has seen, no ear has heard,
no mind has conceived
what God has prepared for those who love him"—
but God has revealed it to us by his Spirit.*
1 Corinthians 2:9-10 NIV

*I did not choose You, but You have chosen me, and ordained
me, that I should go and bring forth fruit, and that my
fruit should remain, that whatever I shall ask of You,
Father, in Jesus' name, You may give it to me.*
John 15:16 PERSONALIZED

HEAVENLY FATHER,

It is an exciting prospect to begin to envision the destiny
You have intended for me. Before I was conceived, You
knew my every step, and even before now You have been
guiding me in the right direction. Things I thought were
coincidental have been contributing to the overall plan.

You declare that I am Your craftmanship, created to do
good deeds, and with Your help I pray those works will
endure. I desire to bear fruit that will remain long after I
am gone and will propagate seed for even more bountiful
produce in the future.

As I go about my days, may I be ever mindful of Your life
flowing through me. Help me to be sensitive to those with
whom I come into contact, offering good spiritual food
from the harvest You've created in me. May it all bring
glory to You.

AMEN.

Discernment

*If you want better insight and discernment, and are searching
for them as you would for lost money or hidden treasure, then
wisdom will be given you, and knowledge of God himself.*
Proverbs 2:3-5 TLB

*The wise heart will know the proper time
and procedure . . . for every matter.*
Ecclesiastes 8:5-6 NIV

*Those who are unspiritual do not receive the gifts of God's
Spirit, for they are foolishness to them, and they are unable
to understand them because they are spiritually discerned.
Those who are spiritual discern all things, and they
are themselves subject to no one else's scrutiny.*
1 Corinthians 2:14-15 NRSV

*Solid food is for the mature, for those whose faculties have
been trained by practice to distinguish good from evil.*
Hebrews 5:14 NRSV

A good tree does not bear corrupt fruit; nor does a corrupt tree bear good fruit, for I'll know every tree by its own fruit.
Luke 6:43-44 PERSONALIZED

ALL-KNOWING FATHER,

With so many voices speaking in the world, it is sometimes difficult to know which voice is Yours. I realize that all that glitters is not gold, and Your Word repeats this fact. Even the devil can appear as an angel of light, so I need to develop a discerning heart.

Most decisions can be pondered over time. When I feel pressured into making quick decisions, help me to step back and take a breath by spending some quiet time with You. There is too much to lose if I move too quickly, but over time a person or a way of living will bear its true fruit. Help me to recognize the fruit by which every situation and every person's life is characterized over the long term so that I can remain safe from harm.

AMEN.

Discipline
Self-discipline

*Not that I have already attained, or am already perfected;
but I press on, that I may lay hold of that for
which Christ Jesus has also laid hold of me.*
Philippians 3:12 NKJV

*God did not give us a spirit of timidity, but
a spirit of power, of love and of self-discipline.*
2 Timothy 1:7 NIV

*By you I can crush a troop,
and by my God I can leap over a wall.*
Psalm 18:29 NRSV

*Since we have so great a cloud of witnesses surrounding us, let
us also lay aside every encumbrance and the sin which so easily
entangles us, and let us run with endurance the race that is set
before us, fixing our eyes on Jesus, the author and perfecter of faith.*
Hebrews 12:1-2 NASB

*Every person who strives for mastery is temperate in
all things. Now they do it to obtain a corruptible crown;
but I an incorruptible crown. . . . I discipline
myself, and bring myself into subjection.*
1 Corinthians 9:25,27 PERSONALIZED

HEAVENLY FATHER,

Personal discipline is not what I would call enjoyable,
especially at the beginning. Doing what comes naturally is
easier; yet this does not bring me closer to You nor produce
good things in my life.

Like a runner in a marathon, I am running in the race
that is my life; but the more I press on, the more Your
strength can take hold and I can gain momentum. I look to
You for help. I can exchange my weakness for the strength
You provide. I'm so thankful that You would say my weakness
is an advantage—I am in a good position to let Your
strength fill my empty places.

Thank You that I do not have to change all areas at once.
Give me the wisdom to know the one area You'd like me to
work on today. And with Your help, I'll get on in the race.

AMEN.

Disciplining Children

If you refuse to discipline your children, it proves
you don't love them; if you love your children,
you will be prompt to discipline them.
Proverbs 13:24 NLT

Folly is bound up in the heart of a boy,
but the rod of discipline drives it far away.
Proverbs 22:15 NRSV

Sometimes mere words are not enough—discipline
is needed. For the words may not be heeded.
Proverbs 29:19 TLB

No discipline is enjoyable while it is happening—
it is painful! But afterward there will be a quiet harvest
of right living for those who are trained in this way.
Hebrews 12:11 NLT

I am to correct my children, and they shall give me rest;
yes, they shall give delight to my soul.
Proverbs 29:17 PERSONALIZED

HEAVENLY FATHER,

Your holy Word states that children are Your blessing to me. Why, then, do they sometimes make life so difficult? There are days it feels like we are living in a war zone and that they are my enemies. I feel guilty for my negative feelings.

Although I realize it is my responsibility to discipline my children and train them up in Your ways, sometimes the task is so exhausting that I want to give in and let them have their own way.

Then I remember that the relationship between You and Jesus is that of Father and Son. And You have great experience with children of all kinds. Surely You can help me to find the right path between firmness and mercy. Beloved Father, I ask You to grant me wisdom and strength to train my children Your way. Enable them to honor me in the way Jesus honors You so we enjoy Your peace.

AMEN.

Discouragement

Hope deferred makes the heart sick,
But when the desire comes, it is a tree of life.
Proverbs 13:12 NKJV

HEAR me when I call, O God of my righteousness:
thou hast enlarged me when I was in distress;
have mercy upon me, and hear my prayer.
Psalm 4:1

This I call to mind and therefore I have hope:
Because of the LORD's great love we are not consumed,
for his compassions never fail.
They are new every morning;
great is your faithfulness.
Lamentations 3:21-23 NIV

The eyes of the LORD move to and fro throughout the earth that
He may strongly support those whose heart is completely His.
2 Chronicles 16:9 NASB

Why are you cast down, O my soul? and why are you disquieted within me? I am to hope in You, God: for I shall yet praise You, who are the health of my countenance, and my God.
Psalm 43:5 PERSONALIZED

GOD OF HOPE,

I'm so thankful for the book of Psalms because I can easily relate to the heart-felt needs the writers experienced. Instead of feeling I am alone in my discouragement, I realize such difficulties are common to all.

David encouraged himself in You, Lord, and he spoke directly to his soul to cheer up. In reality there is never a need to become downcast because I can put my hope in You. You are my sure Foundation, my ever-present Help. Like David, I have never seen the righteous forsaken nor their children begging for bread. There is no situation that You cannot handle and turn around for my good, so I invite You to take over.

Instead of saying, "What am I going to do?" I will begin praising You, for You are truly here. As I stand upon the rock of Your Word, help me to see You are bigger than the problems I face; for that is the reality.

AMEN.

Divorce

Your Creator will be your "husband." The Lord Almighty is
his name; he is your Redeemer, the Holy One of Israel,
the God of all the earth. For the Lord has called you back
from your grief—a young wife abandoned by her husband.
Isaiah 54:5-6 TLB

Let all who take refuge in you rejoice; let them ever sing for joy.
Spread your protection over them, so that
those who love your name may exult in you.
Psalm 5:11 NRSV

Now I know that the LORD saves His anointed;
He will answer him from His holy heaven
With the saving strength of His right hand.
Some trust in chariots, and some in horses;
But we will remember the name of the LORD our God.
Psalm 20:6-7 NKJV

Trust in the LORD, and do good;
Dwell in the land, and feed on His faithfulness.
Delight yourself also in the LORD,
And He shall give you the desires of your heart.
Psalm 37:3-4 NKJV

*You have said to me, "I will never, ever,
leave you, nor forsake you."*
Hebrews 13:5 PERSONALIZED

HEAVENLY FATHER,

My heart is ripped in two, leaving me feeling alone, hurt, and afraid. What will we do now that my husband is gone? Things I once took for granted I now have the responsibility to take care of, and I'm not sure I can do it.

And then there are the children. Am I strong enough to raise them on my own? How can I be both mother and father when I feel like a child myself?

In Your Word, You remind me that You are right here. You have not left me here to fend for myself. You will be a Husband to me and a Father to my children. When I don't know what to do, You will give me the wisdom I need. When it seems we are in a financial crisis, You promise to provide. I need to know that I am loved, Father, and You tell me Your love endures forever.

Help me to forgive and to trust You moment by moment, as You heal me and make me whole again in You.

AMEN.

Divorce
The Effect on My Children

You, O God, do see trouble and grief;
you consider it to take it in hand.
The victim commits himself to you;
you are the helper of the fatherless.
Psalm 10:14 NIV

Restore us, O God;
Cause Your face to shine,
And we shall be saved!
Psalm 80:3 NKJV

In righteousness you will be established;
You will be far from oppression, for you will not fear;
And from terror, for it will not come near you.
Isaiah 54:14 NASB

Those who fear the LORD are secure;
he will be a place of refuge for their children.
Proverbs 14:26 NLT

You are a father of my fatherless children.
Psalm 68:5 PERSONALIZED

HEAVENLY FATHER,

I come to You on behalf of my children, asking You to show Yourself strong in their behalf. It is not their fault that their father is gone, so I ask You to help me to reassure them. Please mend their broken hearts and dreams and give them hope for a brighter day. I ask You to reveal Yourself to them as their Father, One on whom they can rely, One who will never forsake them. May You reveal to them the depth of Your love, giving them a firm foundation from which to grow.

And help me too, Lord, to not add to the problem. No matter what my ex-husband has done, he is still my children's father. Help me to exercise self-control and to not tear him down in their eyes. Even though he has hurt me, I refuse to add to their pain. Give me Your strength and wisdom, dear Lord. And father my children, please.

AMEN.

Encouragement

I lift up my eyes to the hills—
where does my help come from?
My help comes from the LORD,
the Maker of heaven and earth.
Psalm 121:1-2 NIV

When I pray, you answer me, and encourage
me by giving me the strength I need.
Psalm 138:3 TLB

We do not lose heart. . . . For our light and
momentary troubles are achieving for us an
eternal glory that far outweighs them all.
2 Corinthians 4:16-17 NIV

The things you have learned and received and heard and seen in
me, practice these things, and the God of peace will be with you.
Philippians 4: 9 NASB

Now to You who are able to do exceeding abundantly
above all that I ask or imagine, according to
Your power that works in me, to You be glory!
Ephesians 3:20-21 PERSONALIZED

ENCOURAGING FATHER,

What an encouragement it is to realize that Your dreams for me are even greater than anything I could conceive of for myself. When I look at my life, I am tempted to see it only through human eyes, yet You offer me optimistic insight.

I ask You to forgive me for limiting my vision and for the pessimism to which I've fallen prey. Seeing my life as ordinary and unimportant must grieve Your heart, when You have provided such riches for me. I want to take the limits off my imagination and give You full reign, so You can accomplish Your desires through me.

I ask You to help me avail myself of Your mighty power within me and not to hinder it in any way. Only You can expand my vision and open me to new things You have for me. I am encouraged as I look to You and begin to think Your Heavenly thoughts.

AMEN.

Enthusiasm

Never be lazy in your work but serve the Lord enthusiastically.
Romans 12:11 TLB

Having started the ball rolling so enthusiastically, you should carry this project through to completion just as gladly, giving whatever you can out of whatever you have. Let your enthusiastic idea at the start be equalled by your realistic action now.
2 Corinthians 8:11 TLB

He died under God's judgment against our sins, so that he could rescue us from constant falling into sin and make us his very own people, with cleansed hearts and real enthusiasm for doing kind things for others.
Titus 2:14 TLB

MAKE a joyful shout to the LORD, all you lands!
Serve the LORD with gladness;
Come before His presence with singing.
Psalm 100:1-2 NKJV

*I'm to love You, the LORD my God, and to walk in all Your
ways, and to keep Your commandments, and to adhere to
You, and to serve You with all my heart and with all my soul.*
Joshua 22:5 PERSONALIZED

JOYFUL GOD,

It seems like the whole world wants to experience enthusiasm, and we look to many things to provide a quick fix. Numb from so many of life's disappointments, most of us seek temporary pleasure to give us a feeling of life and vitality. But it doesn't take very long to realize the feeling merely passes.

Father, even many of Your children are glum instead of joyful. Settling for a religion of shoulds and should nots, we all seem to miss the point.

When I realize that *enthusiasm* comes from *en theos*, words meaning "in God," I begin to get a glimpse into the life You have for me. Life in You is what it's really all about, a well of life springing up within me. Knowing You is something to be enthusiastic about, as there is no end to Your goodness. Help me to learn how to draw from this well of Your salvation, and as I drink to my fill, help me to share this enthusiasm with others, whetting their appetites to know You.

AMEN.

Eternal Life

"God so loved the world that he gave his only Son,
so that everyone who believes in him may
not perish but may have eternal life."
John 3:16 NRSV

I count all things to be loss in view of the surpassing value
of knowing Christ Jesus my Lord, for whom I have
suffered the loss of all things, and count them
but rubbish in order that I may gain Christ.
Philippians 3:8 NASB

We know that the Son of God has come and has given us
an understanding, that we may know Him who is true;
and we are in Him who is true, in His Son Jesus Christ.
This is the true God and eternal life.
1 John 5:20 NKJV

He will give eternal life to those who patiently do
the will of God, seeking for the unseen glory
and honor and eternal life that he offers.
Romans 2:7 TLB

*This is eternal life: that I might know You, the only
true God, and Jesus Christ, whom You have sent.*
John 17:3 PERSONALIZED

EVERLASTING FATHER,

It is wonderful to know that You love me so much that
You sent the only Son You had to die in my place. The
moment I received Him, eternal life began within me.
What a blessing it is that I don't have to wait till I get to
Heaven to partake of this marvelous life. I can experience
it now.

Jesus said that eternal life is to know You and to know
Him whom You sent. The apostle Paul counted all the
blessings of his life as loss in order to know You.

Give me a passion, like Jesus had, to be with You also.
Give me a spirit of wisdom and revelation, flooding the
eyes of my heart with light that I may know You and the
hope of Your calling. And as I know You more intimately
each day, I pray You will give me opportunities to introduce
others to you, Life Eternal.

AMEN.

Example

You yourselves are our letter, written on our
hearts, known and read by everybody.
2 Corinthians 3:2 NIV

Don't be tyrants, but lead them by your good example,
and when the Head Shepherd comes, your reward
will be a never-ending share in his glory and honor.
1 Peter 5:3-4 TLB

Follow God's example in everything you do just as a much
loved child imitates his father. Be full of love for others,
following the example of Christ who loved you and gave
himself to God as a sacrifice to take away your sins.
Ephesians 5:1-2 TLB

In all things show yourself to be an example of
good deeds, with purity in doctrine, dignified.
Titus 2:7 NASB

I'm to be an example to the believers, in word, in
conversation, in charity, in spirit, in faith, in purity.
1 Timothy 4:12 PERSONALIZED

HEAVENLY FATHER,

There is no place more important for me to set an example as a believer than in my own home. Yet when I leave the security of my abode to go out into the world, I need to be mindful as well.

The apostle Paul said that as a believer I am a living letter from God to them, known and read by all people. Wherever I go, someone is "reading" me. I realize that I may be the only Bible many will ever read, so I pray that I will represent You well. I ask You to help me be aware of others and to give them something positive to read. May the law of kindness be on my lips; may my words be seasoned with grace.

As I conduct my affairs, may others see Jesus living in me. Help me to love as You love, to have faith, and to walk in purity that You may be glorified in me.

AMEN.

Failure

Now change your mind and attitude to God and turn to him
so he can cleanse away your sins and send you wonderful
times of refreshment from the presence of the Lord.
Acts 3:19 TLB

We know that all things work together for good for those
who love God, who are called according to his purpose.
Romans 8:28 NRSV

I let it all out;
I said, "I'll make a clean breast of my failures to GOD."
Suddenly the pressure was gone—
my guilt dissolved,
my sin disappeared.
Psalm 32:5 THE MESSAGE

He brought me up out of the pit
of destruction, out of the miry clay,
And He set my feet upon a rock making
my footsteps firm.
Psalm 40:2 NASB

LORD, *You uphold me when I fall and*
raise me up when I am bowed down.
Psalm 145:14 PERSONALIZED

UNDERSTANDING FATHER,

My faults and failures loom before me, casting a long
shadow over my life. How could I have been so foolish to
think that I could succeed? Setting out in my own human
efforts, I have fallen and feel unable to recover.

Then You get my attention; I look up and see Your face. I
hear You gently call me to reach out and take Your hand.
"Look up," You say in a reassuring voice, "for I am here to
help. It's not half as bad as you think it is, for I am not
through with this thing yet."

Your blessings lead to repentance, and You've proven it
once again. When you offer to help me in my troubles, my
heart opens up, longing to be right with You once more.
Father, I ask You to forgive me for my failures and my
faults. I receive Your cleansing forgiveness and restoring
love to walk with You afresh.

AMEN.

Faith
In God's Word

I am watching to see that my word is fulfilled.
Jeremiah 1:12 NIV

The LORD exists forever; your word is firmly fixed in heaven.
Psalm 119:89 NRSV

O Lord GOD, Thou art God, and Thy words are truth,
and Thou hast promised this good thing to Thy servant.
2 Samuel 7:28 NASB

He has given us both his promise and his oath, two things we
can completely count on, for it is impossible for God to tell a lie.
Hebrews 6:18 TLB

"Heaven and earth will pass away,
but my words will not pass away."
Matthew 24:35 NRSV

*Like Abraham I'm not to waver at Your promise
through unbelief, God, but to be strong in faith,
giving glory to You; being fully persuaded that, what
You have promised, You are able also to perform.*
Romans 4:20-21 Personalized

Faithful God,

It is a great reassurance that You are not a human who lies. No matter how well meaning I am, there are times I have broken my word. But unlike those of fallible humans, Your promises never fail. You watch over every single word You have spoken to ensure it comes true.

Help me to be more like Abraham and simply take You at Your Word. Instead of allowing my mind to race, swirling around with doubts and questions, help me to still myself and remember once again that You are God and You mean what You say. You bound Yourself with an oath, so why should I fret?

Father, I give You all my doubts and fears and begin afresh today. Strengthen me in my faith as I give glory to You and exalt You in all things. Help me to grow to be fully convinced that what You have promised You are also able to perform.

Amen.

Faith

Confidence God Hears My Prayers

Know that the LORD has set apart the faithful for himself;
the LORD hears when I call to him.
Psalm 4:3 NRSV

It will also come to pass
that before they call, I will answer;
and while they are still speaking, I will hear.
Isaiah 65:24 NASB

"If you abide in Me, and My words abide in you, you will
ask what you desire, and it shall be done for you."
John 15:7 NKJV

"I say to you: Ask and it will be given to you;
seek and you will find; knock and the door will be opened
to you. For everyone who asks receives; he who seeks finds;
and to him who knocks, the door will be opened."
Luke 11:9-10 NIV

*This is the confidence that I have in You, that, if I ask
any thing according to Your will, You hear me; and if
I know that You hear me, whatever I ask, I know
that I have the petitions that I desired of You.*
1 John 5:14 PERSONALIZED

HEAVENLY FATHER,

So many times I have concerns, but I fail to even bring
them to You in prayer. I find myself thinking, *Why bother?
Who am I? My prayers won't do any good anyway.*

But this is where I have been wrong. You tell me to have
confidence when I pray, and You have told me how. First, I
must ask according to Your will, and You have given me
Your will in Your holy written Word. If I bring one of Your
promises before You, You promise You will hear me. Then,
You reassure me that I can be confident I have the requests
that I ask of You. Furthermore, You have forgiven me and
made me righteous in Christ. Then, You tell me that the
effectual, fervent prayers of righteous people avail much.
What a gracious Father You are!

Please direct me to promises regarding the things on my
mind, and I will rest in confidence as You perform Your
Word on my behalf.

AMEN.

Family Life

Unless the LORD builds the house,
those who build it labor in vain.
Psalm 127:1 NRSV

Your wife will be like a fruitful vine
within your house;
your sons will be like olive shoots
around your table.
Thus is the man blessed
who fears the LORD.
Psalm 128:3-4 NIV

Grandchildren are the crown of the aged,
and the glory of children is their parents.
Proverbs 17:6 NRSV

Behold, children are a gift of the LORD . . .
How blessed is the man whose quiver is full of them.
Psalm 127:3-5 NASB

*Through wisdom is my house built; and by understanding
it is established; and by knowledge shall my chambers
be filled with all precious and pleasant riches.*
Proverbs 24:3-4 PERSONALIZED

HEAVENLY FATHER,

When I realize that You instituted the family long before
You began the Church, I stand in awe at Your marvelous
plan. You love relationships and have designed the family as
a place of refuge in this troublesome world.

But families are complex entities, made up of complex
individuals. Each member in the family is a unique and
priceless being, individually created by You for Your
purpose. No member of the family is less valuable than any
other, yet together we are far more effective than we could
ever be on our own.

So I ask You for wisdom to help us build a family that
brings glory to You. Give us the understanding we need to
work together as a harmonious symphony. Bring this
knowledge across our paths so that we will overflow with
rich blessings for others and can offer them a place of
refuge as well.

AMEN.

Fatigue

Remember the Sabbath day by keeping it holy. Six days you
shall labor and do all your work, but the seventh day is a Sabbath
to the LORD your God. On it you shall not do any work.
Exodus 20:8-10 NIV

Return, O my soul, to your rest,
for the LORD has dealt bountifully with you.
Psalm 116:7 NRSV

It is vain for you to rise up early,
To sit up late,
To eat the bread of sorrows;
For so He gives His beloved sleep.
Psalm 127:2 NKJV

You chart the path ahead of me and
tell me where to stop and rest.
Psalm 139:3 TLB

*I'm to come to You, I who labor and am heavy laden, and You
will give me rest. I'm to take Your yoke upon me, and learn
of You; for You are meek and humble in heart; and I shall find
rest for my soul, for Your yoke is easy, and Your burden is light.*
Matthew 11:28-30 PERSONALIZED

ALMIGHTY FATHER,

I'm so tired and weary that sometimes I don't know how
I will continue. It seems that I've been in perpetual motion
for such a long time, till now I'm depleted of all strength
and fatigue has set in. So many areas of my life need attention, stretching me thin, and still there's more to deal with;
but I must stop and rest.

All along the journey that You have charted for my life,
You have set interludes for calm and quiet to provide still-
ness for my mind. My Shepherd, You beckon, "Come to
Me," and You will give me rest. Refreshing and reviving me,
You restore my sense of well-being. Sweet sleep for my
body gives me a fresh outlook.

Help me, Lord, to sense when it's time for a break. As I
pause to wait on You, You assure me that You will renew my
strength, bearing me up like an eagle, to continue on again.

AMEN.

Fear

I sought the LORD, and He answered me,
And delivered me from all my fears.
Psalm 34:4 NASB

With [wisdom and common sense] on guard you can sleep
without fear; you need not be afraid of disaster or the plots of
wicked men, for the Lord is with you; he protects you.
Proverbs 3:24-26 TLB

Encourage those who are afraid. Tell them,
"Be strong, fear not, for your God is coming to
destroy your enemies. He is coming to save you."
Isaiah 35:4 TLB

Fear not, for I have redeemed you;
I have called you by your name;
You are Mine.
Isaiah 43:1 NKJV

I am not to fear; for You are with me. I am not to be dismayed; for
You are my God. You will strengthen me; yes, You will help me;
yes, You will uphold me with the right hand of Your righteousness.
Isaiah 41:10 PERSONALIZED

HEAVENLY FATHER,

Your Word tells me not to be afraid, but sometimes fear seizes me suddenly, paralyzing me in its grip. I find I am unable to turn it off at will.

Perhaps preventive maintenance is the key. Since this is a mental battle, I will call to mind Your promises: You are with me, You help me, and You promise to make me strong. You say that You have not given me a spirit of fear but one of power, love, and a sound mind. I pray that You will help me to take hold of that power and live in a constant awareness of Your love. Your love makes my fear evaporate, and You ease my troubled mind.

"Jesus loves me, this I know, for the Bible tells me so." When I dwell on this lyric, I think, *What fear could possibly overcome this truth?* It seems the first Bible song I ever learned is one I can still live by.

AMEN.

Finances

Giving

"Whatever measure you use in giving—large or small—
it will be used to measure what is given back to you."
Luke 6:38 NLT

*He who is gracious to a poor man lends to the L*ORD,
And He will repay him for his good deed.
Proverbs 19:17 NASB

Bring all the tithes into the storehouse so that there
will be food enough in my Temple; if you do, I will open
up the windows of heaven for you and pour out a blessing
so great you won't have room enough to take it in!
Try it! Let me prove it to you!
Malachi 3:10 TLB

Every man shall give as he is able, according to the blessing
*of the L*ORD *your God which He has given you.*
Deuteronomy 16:17 NKJV

God, You love a cheerful giver.
2 Corinthians 9:7 PERSONALIZED

GENEROUS FATHER,

I used to have an erroneous idea regarding financial giving. I saw it as a burden, something I *had* to do; however, Your Word changes my point of view. You say that it is more blessed to give than it is to receive, and the joy that giving provides me is a reward in itself.

When I realize that You promise to supply all my needs, I need not be concerned that my well will ever run dry. You say You are unwilling to do without a cheerful giver, so I am confident You will always provide something that I can contribute.

The Bible promises that when I give, it will be given back to me in greater quantity than I gave, and even to an over-flowing abundance. Understanding this gives me even more incentive, for it is clear that You want to bless me in return.

To whom or in what area would You have me contribute financially today?

AMEN.

Finances
God's Provision

"Do not keep striving for what you are to eat and what
you are to drink, and do not keep worrying. For it is
the nations of the world that strive after all these
things, and your Father knows that you need them."
Luke 12:29-30 NRSV

I will give you regular rains, and the land will yield
bumper crops, and the trees will be loaded with fruit long
after the normal time! And grapes will still be ripening
when sowing time comes again. You shall eat your fill.
Leviticus 26:4-5 TLB

I will abundantly bless her provision;
I will satisfy her needy with bread.
Psalm 132:15 NASB

I have been young, and now am old;
yet have I not seen the righteous forsaken,
nor his seed begging bread.
Psalm 37:25 KJV

*You, my God, shall supply all my need according
to Your riches in glory in Christ Jesus.*
Philippians 4:19 PERSONALIZED

FAITHFUL FATHER,

If ever there was a piece of good news, this promise is certainly it. No matter what financial situations confront me today, You vowed to supply *all* my needs. The best part of this news is that it is according to *Your* riches in glory in Christ Jesus. It is not according to my job; it is not according to my husband's benefit package. It is not dependent upon an earthly inheritance or the stock market and Wall Street.

No, the only thing I need to know is that regardless of my circumstances, be they good or be they bad, You own the cattle on a thousand hills and Your streets are paved with gold. My miniscule needs are certainly not too much for You.

You care for the tiny sparrows, and You even know the number of hairs that are on my head. Since You are so awesome, my God, I will not be concerned with where the provision will come from or how You will provide it. I will simply put my trust in You.

AMEN.

Finances
Our Responsibility

The good leave an inheritance to their children's children.
Proverbs 13:22 NRSV

Anyone who won't care for his own relatives when they need
help, especially those living in his own family, has no right to
say he is a Christian. Such a person is worse than the heathen.
1 Timothy 5:8 TLB

Owe no one anything except to love one another,
for he who loves another has fulfilled the law.
Romans 13:8 NKJV

Just as farm workers who plow fields and thresh
the grain expect a share of the harvest, Christian
workers should be paid by those they serve.
1 Corinthians 9:10 NLT

[If I am a good steward, in that day You will say to me,]
"Well done, you good and faithful servant. You have been
faithful over a few things; I will make you ruler over
many things. Enter into the joy of your lord."
Matthew 25:21 PERSONALIZED

HEAVENLY FATHER,

I am thankful I can trust You to fulfill all of our family's monetary needs; however, I am mindful that I have certain financial responsibilities.

- Help me to offer the first portion of my earnings to You.
- Help me to provide for our family's needs.
- This is the hardest, Lord. Living within my means is good stewardship of all You've entrusted to me. Help me to say no to myself when catalogs and store displays tempt me.
- Staying current on all bills shows I am a person of integrity. Help me to do this.
- May I give to those less fortunate to share in Your mercy.
- Supporting overseas missions helps to spread the Good News. Guide me to the right ministry to support.

Thank You for not giving me these obligations to shoulder without Your help. Please give me wisdom, so I can fulfill my responsibilities in ways that please You.

AMEN.

Forgiving Myself

Be gentle with one another, sensitive. Forgive one another
as quickly and thoroughly as God in Christ forgave you.
Ephesians 4:32 THE MESSAGE

I trusted in your steadfast love;
my heart shall rejoice in your salvation.
I will sing to the LORD,
because he has dealt bountifully with me.
Psalm 13:5-6 NRSV

Surely goodness and love will follow me all the days of
my life, and I will dwell in the house of the LORD forever.
Psalm 23:6 NIV

I will be glad and rejoice in Your mercy,
For You have considered my trouble;
You have known my soul in adversities,
And have not shut me up into the hand of the enemy;
You have set my feet in a wide place.
Psalm 31:7-8 NKJV

I am to love my neighbor as myself.
Matthew 19:19 PERSONALIZED

LOVING FATHER,

I am quite willing to forgive those who wrong me; however, my challenge is in forgiving myself. Somehow forgiving others seems easy compared to letting myself off the hook. I tend to hang on to condemnation, almost as though I feel obligated to punish myself for my wrongs. Even after I am assured that You and others have forgiven me, I still harbor a grudge against myself.

Maybe it is because when I forgive others, I am hopeful it won't happen again. However, where I am concerned, I'm painfully aware of my shortcomings and know I'm likely to sin again.

I am coming to realize how unhealthy this attitude is. Help me to respond to myself the way that You do. Your mercies are new every morning, and You cast my sins away as far as the east is from the west. Who am I to respond differently?

Help me today, Lord, to love myself as I love my neighbors, forgiving myself and remembering the errors no more.

AMEN.

Forgiving Others

Peter came to him and asked, "Lord, how often should
I forgive someone who sins against me? Seven times?"
"No!" Jesus replied, "seventy times seven!"
Matthew 18:21-22 NLT

"Watch yourselves. If your brother sins, rebuke
him, and if he repents, forgive him."
Luke 17:3 NIV

"Blessed are the merciful,
for they shall receive mercy."
Matthew 5:7 NASB

"Be merciful, just as your Father is merciful."
Luke 6:36 NRSV

*When I stand praying, I am to forgive if I have anything
against anyone that You, Father, who are in heaven,
also may forgive me my trespasses.*
Mark 11:25 PERSONALIZED

LOVING FATHER,

Forgiving others can be difficult when the transgressions
against me hurt. When the sins of others leave me feeling
worthless, my emotions erupt. I make an honest attempt
to forgive; yet the feelings stick, and I can't quite shake
them loose.

Perhaps this is why Jesus said I would have to forgive
seventy time seven. He knew that at times it would seem
like the transgressions I have forgiven ricochet and come
right back at me. I toss the hurts over on You, only to have
them return.

Forgiving others allows You to forgive me and that motivates me as I struggle. And in my heart, I want to forgive. I
ask for Your grace to help my emotions subside as I pardon
others. Help me to love them as You do.

AMEN.

Future

Heaven

Surely there is a hereafter,
And your hope will not be cut off.
Proverbs 23:18 NKJV

The Lord Himself will descend from heaven with a shout,
with the voice of the archangel and with the trumpet
of God, and the dead in Christ will rise first. Then we
who are alive and remain will be caught up together
with them in the clouds to meet the Lord in the air.
1 Thessalonians 4:16-17 NASB

He will wipe every tear from their eyes. There will be
no more death or mourning or crying or pain.
Revelation 21:4 NIV

The throne of God and of the Lamb will be in it, and his
servants will worship him; they will see his face. . . . There will
be no more night; they need no light of lamp or sun, for the Lord
God will be their light, and they will reign forever and ever.
Revelation 22:3-5 NRSV

In Your house, Father, are many mansions; if it were not so, You would have told me. You are going to prepare a place for me.
John 14:2 PERSONALIZED

HEAVENLY FATHER,

It is easy to forget about the reality of Heaven when I get caught up in the affairs of daily life. But no matter what challenges I face during my earthly pilgrimage, they are fleeting in comparison to the glorious eternity I will spend with You.

A day in Your courts is better than a thousand anywhere else. I am a citizen of Heaven, simply passing through this earthly life. In my heart is a longing for Heaven, homesickness for the place Jesus has prepared for me, for it is my true home.

In that place there will be no more sorrow, no more tears, and Your glorious light will never cease to shine. I will be forever reunited with those I love who have gone before me, and we will spend eternity worshiping around Your throne.

Help me to keep this hope before me, to stay on course, undistracted by the world's riches and entertainments.

AMEN.

Future

My Future

*Look at those who are honest and good,
for a wonderful future lies before those who love peace.*
Psalm 37:37 NLT

*Since the Lord is directing our steps, why try to
understand everything that happens along the way?*
Proverbs 20:24 TLB

*The path of the just is like the shining sun,
That shines ever brighter unto the perfect day.*
Proverbs 4:18 NKJV

*You were called for the very purpose
that you might inherit a blessing.*
1 Peter 3:9 NASB

*You know the thoughts that You think of me, thoughts of
peace and not of evil, to give me a future and a hope.*
Jeremiah 29:11 PERSONALIZED

FAITHFUL FATHER,

I'm afraid of the future. Like Peter walking on the water,
I do just fine for a while. But as soon as I take my eyes off
You, I begin to sink.

You reached out Your hand to Peter and rescued him.
Reach out to me and steady my sinking emotions. Help me
to see Your faithful hand in Your promises.

Let those promises be the solid rock on which I can
stand. You have plans for my good, not my calamity or
destruction. These plans give me hope, dispelling my
darkest fears. Even if I walk through the valley of the
shadow of death, You will be with me, giving me the grace
that I need to come through safely. No enemy's weapon
formed against me can prosper, so I can rest assured that
any threats to my future will fall helplessly to the ground.

Thank You for securing me in Your promises.

AMEN.

Future
Prayer for My Children to Fulfill Their Destiny

Before I made you in your mother's womb, I chose you.
Before you were born, I set you apart for a special work.
Jeremiah 1:5 NCV

Direct my steps by Your word,
And let no iniquity have dominion over me.
Psalm 119:133 NKJV

The human mind plans the way,
but the LORD directs the steps.
Proverbs 16:9 NRSV

Commit everything you do to the Lord.
Trust him to help you do it and he will.
Psalm 37:5 TLB

All my children shall be taught of You, LORD;
and great shall be the peace of my children.
Isaiah 54:13 PERSONALIZED

OMNISCIENT FATHER,

You promise to show me things to come, so I ask You to give me insight into my children's future. I pray that their spiritual eyes would be flooded with light that they might know the hope to which You've called them.

You have specific plans in mind for each one of them; please make me sensitive to those plans. Help me to discover the bent You have given each one, and show me ways I can nurture their gifts, so they will bear much fruit. Help me train my children to live the way You intended for them so that when they are older, they will not depart from Your path.

Surround my children with Godly friends and relationships, and protect them from evil influences that would cause them to stray. May they fulfill their destinies and live lives that glorify You.

AMEN.

Future
Prayer for My Children's Marriages

I am the LORD your God,
who teaches you to profit,
Who leads you in the way you should go.
Isaiah 48:17 NASB

My son, honey whets the appetite, and so does wisdom!
When you enjoy becoming wise, there is hope for you!
A bright future lies ahead!
Proverbs 24:13 TLB

The wise are cautious and turn away from evil,
but the fool throws off restraint and is careless.
Proverbs 14:16 NRSV

The fear of the LORD is life indeed;
filled with it one rests secure
and suffers no harm.
Proverbs 19:23 NRSV

*I'm to hold marriage honorable among all,
and the marriage bed undefiled.*
Hebrews 13:4 PERSONALIZED

WISE FATHER,

The choice of their mates is one of the single most significant decisions my children can make. With divorce running rampant, I want to cover their future marriages with prayer.

I pray that my relationship with my mate will set a good example of Your plan for husband and wife. Where we stumble, teach my children what is right. I pray for the individuals my children may someday marry to be raised in Godly homes with healthy relationships as well.

I pray that You will protect my children and their future mates from seducing spirits that would entrap them through the flattering words of others. Give my children the spiritual fortitude to resist temptation and to save their sexual expression for marriage. Help them to see the benefit of waiting.

I pray You will protect my children and future in-laws from tragedy and abuse. Thank You for giving Your angels charge over them to protect them in all their ways.

AMEN.

Godly Living

Put on the Lord Jesus Christ, and make no provision
for the flesh, to gratify its desires.
Romans 13:14 NRSV

Put on the new man which was created according
to God, in true righteousness and holiness.
Ephesians 4:24 NKJV

The grace of God that brings salvation has appeared to all men,
teaching us that, denying ungodliness and worldly lusts, we
should live soberly, righteously, and godly in the present age.
Titus 2:11-12 NKJV

Have nothing to do with godless myths and old
wives' tales; rather, train yourself to be godly.
1 Timothy 4:7 NIV

I am not to be conformed to this world; but I am to be transformed by the renewing of my mind, that I may prove what is that good, acceptable, and perfect will of God.
Romans 12:2 PERSONALIZED

MY LORD,

Living life as one of Your children is the most fulfilling part of my life. Loving Your holy Word and Your infinite ways gives my life purpose and meaning.

Unfortunately, there are times when my heart is divided within me, and I find myself drawn to the things this world offers. Perhaps this is what Jesus meant when He said that the spirit is willing but the flesh is weak.

I am wholly committed to my new life in You, so help me, holy Lord, to take one situation at a time. As I confront each new circumstance that tempts me into conforming to this world, I pray that Your Holy Spirit would guide me and strengthen me to do things in ways that please You. May I daily become more and more like Jesus.

AMEN.

God's Love

*God is love. When we take up permanent residence
in a life of love, we live in God and God lives in us.*
1 John 4:16 THE MESSAGE

*Jesus knew that the time had come for him to leave this
world and go to the Father. Having loved his own who were
in the world, he now showed them the full extent of his love.*
John 13:1 NIV

*"If anyone loves Me, he will keep My word; and
My Father will love him, and We will come
to him, and make Our abode with him."*
John 14:23 NASB

*"As the Father has loved me, so I have loved you; abide
in my love. If you keep my commandments, you will
abide in my love, just as I have kept my Father's
commandments and abide in his love."*
John 15:9-10 NRSV

I'm to behold what manner of love You have bestowed upon me, Father, that I should be called Your child; therefore the world does not know me because it did not know You.
1 John 3:1 PERSONALIZED

LOVING FATHER,

I pray as Paul prayed: that I may have roots and foundation in Your love, so that I, along with all of Your people, may have the power to understand how broad and long, how high and deep, is Christ's love for me. May I come to know His unfathomable love so that I may be completely filled with Your very nature, O God. (See Ephesians 3:17-19 TEV).

Only when I am conscious of Your great love for me can I love others as You do, Father, and only then can I love my neighbor as I also love myself.

It is a signal to a blind world that I am a follower of You when I love other Christians. You've channeled this love through my heart, so I ask You to help me learn to express it, loving others the way Jesus loves me.

Thank You for Your great love that chases away my fears and makes me whole in Christ.

AMEN.

God's Nature

Because the LORD your God is a merciful God, he will
neither abandon you nor destroy you; he will not forget
the covenant with your ancestors that he swore to them.
Deuteronomy 4:31 NRSV

The LORD your God is the God of gods and the
Lord of lords, the great, the mighty, and the awesome
God who does not show partiality nor take a bribe.
Deuteronomy 10:17 NASB

Behold, God is mine helper:
the Lord is with them that uphold my soul.
Psalm 54:4 KJV

To You, O my Strength, I will sing praises;
For God is my defense,
My God of mercy.
Psalm 59:17 NKJV

*How excellent is Your lovingkindness to me, O God! Therefore
all humankind takes refuge under the shadow of Your wings.*
Psalm 36:7 PERSONALIZED

MERCIFUL FATHER,

I think the enemy's predominant scheme against me is to
deceive me about Your nature. He tries to get me to ques-
tion the genuineness of Your love for me, painting You as a
not-too-nice Person, someone looking to dominate me.

But when I come to You with my questions, You reveal
Your true goodness. You reassure me saying, "I am Love."
You don't just *have* love—You *are* Love. You give me Your
favor for a lifetime. You are not bad—You are good; and
Your mercy endures forever. Jesus shows me Your nature,
for He is gentle and humble in heart, not harsh and full
of arrogance.

Thank You for Your many precious promises to me. As I
partake of them, I am able to trust You more, and then I
become more like you, loving and gentle. The gentle Christ
lives in me and brings about a change in me that gives me
hope I will one day be like You.

AMEN.

Gossip

The tongue is a small thing, but what enormous damage it can do. A great forest can be set on fire by one tiny spark.
James 3:5 TLB

A gossip reveals secrets;
therefore do not associate with a babbler.
Proverbs 20:19 NRSV

This should be your ambition: to live a quiet life, minding your own business and doing your own work.
1 Thessalonians 4:11 TLB

Lord, who may go and find refuge and shelter
in your tabernacle up on your holy hill?
. . . Anyone who refuses to slander others, does
not listen to gossip, never harms his neighbor.
Psalm 15:1,3 TLB

A perverse person sows strife; and a gossip separates best friends.
Proverbs 16:28 PERSONALIZED

HEAVENLY FATHER,

Gossip is an insidious force, which can separate the best
of friends as it spreads around its deadly venom. Help me
to be a trustworthy person who will quiet destructive tales,
not one who sows seeds of strife. The one with loose lips is
described as an evil person, and I want to avoid evil. Just as
a fire goes out for lack of fuel, tensions will disappear if I
refuse to participate in gossip. Help me to do that.

The tongue is a powerful weapon, which can be wielded
for good or for evil, and I want to train mine in the Godly
way. I ask You to help put a guard over my lips, so I will
not bring reproach upon Your kingdom nor prove myself
untrustworthy.

I ask You to forgive me for the times I have participated
in the rumor mill and to help me be an example of a faithful friend and follower of You.

AMEN.

Grace

All have sinned and fall short of the glory of God,
being justified as a gift by His grace through
the redemption which is in Christ Jesus.
Romans 3:23-24 NASB

Where sin abounded, grace abounded much more, so that
as sin reigned in death, even so grace might reign through
righteousness to eternal life through Jesus Christ our Lord.
Romans 5:20-21 NKJV

In him we have redemption through his blood, the forgiveness
of sins, in accordance with the riches of God's grace.
Ephesians 1:7 NIV

You know the grace of our Lord Jesus Christ, that though
He was rich, yet for your sakes He became poor,
that you through His poverty might become rich.
2 Corinthians 8:9 NKJV

*By grace I am saved through faith; and that grace
is not from me; it is the gift of God; not of
works done by me, in case I should boast.*
Ephesians 2:8-9 PERSONALIZED

GENEROUS FATHER,

I've heard it said that grace is Your unmerited favor,
meaning there is nothing I can do to deserve the love You
have for me; but the world I live in operates by an opposite
set of rules. I exercise to lose weight, I invest to receive a
return, and in order to have friends, I must first show
myself friendly.

Yet I love You because You first loved me. Your Son
became poor that I might be rich, sick that I might be well.
He became sin that I could be made righteous and died so
that I might live. Nothing I could ever do could qualify me
for such blessings.

Because You have so bountifully showered me with grace,
I pray You will give me opportunities to extend this blessing to others. Help me to love those who are unable to love
me, and lead me to people in need who could never repay
me. Help me to be a light to the world.

AMEN.

Grief
Death of Spouse

A defender of widows,
is God in his holy dwelling.
Psalm 68:5 NIV

The LORD . . . relieves the fatherless and widow.
Psalm 146:9 NKJV

The LORD will tear down the proud person's house.
But he will protect property of a widow.
Proverbs 15:25 NCV

I will give them
the oil of gladness to replace their sorrow . . .
[and] clothes of praise to replace their spirit of sadness.
Isaiah 61:3 NCV

*I am to fear not; for I shall not be ashamed. Neither should
I be perplexed, for I shall not be put to shame . . . I shall
not remember the reproach of my widowhood anymore.
For You, my Maker, are my husband; the LORD of hosts
is Your name, my Redeemer, the Holy One of Israel.*
Isaiah 54:4-5 PERSONALIZED

COMFORTING FATHER,

I did not know it was possible to feel so lost and alone.
Leaving a gaping hole, part of me has been torn away. I
always thought we would grow old together. "Till death do
you part" was supposed to mean somewhere way off in the
future, but this is where I find myself now.

Why did he go away? Even though I know it wasn't his
fault, still something in me feels angry that he has left me
here to shoulder all the responsibilities on my own. At
times I feel numb, and then a sudden wave of sadness
almost swallows me whole.

But as I reach out to You, You draw close to me. Your
presence envelops me as I let go and weep. You will not
leave me without comfort or help; and though I sow in
tears now, You reassure me there is joy in my future. Give
me the grace to move on, one day at a time.

AMEN.

Grief
Change or Other Loss

My times are in Your hand.
Psalm 31:15 NKJV

*Whatever is good and perfect comes to us from God
above, who created all heaven's lights. Unlike them,
he never changes or casts shifting shadows.*
James 1:17 NLT

*Happy are those who make
the LORD their trust.*
Psalm 40:4 NRSV

*They that trust in the LORD
shall be as mount Zion,
which cannot be removed, but abideth for ever.*
Psalm 125:1 KJV

To everything in my life there is a season, and a time
to every purpose of mine under the heaven . . .
A time for me to weep, and a time for me to laugh;
a time for me to mourn, and a time for me to dance.
Ecclesiastes 3:1,4 PERSONALIZED

FAITHFUL FATHER,

Although I know change is an inevitable part of life, that doesn't necessarily make it any easier. Letting go can be very difficult. Maybe I'm a creature of habit and don't like to be moved out of my comfort zone.

"Forgetting those things which are behind and reaching forward to those things which are ahead" (Philippians 3:13 NKJV) takes courage, and I'm not sure I'm ready. Will I like this new thing You are doing? I guess it comes down to trust. I know it's okay to grieve over the things I'm leaving behind, but to grieve too long is to rebel, to accuse You of being evil and not good. Help me look forward with a positive expectation to what You have for me.

Each season in life comes with its own unique blessings and challenges. Forgive me for taking the previous season for granted, and help me to celebrate the good things ahead.

AMEN.

Grief
Loss of a Child

The LORD has heard the voice of my weeping.
The LORD has heard my supplication;
The LORD will receive my prayer.
Psalm 6:8-9 NKJV

"The thief comes only to steal and kill and destroy; I have
come that they may have life, and have it to the full."
John 10:10 NIV

We have not an high priest which cannot be touched
with the feeling of our infirmities; but was in all points
tempted like as we are, yet without sin.
Hebrews 4:15 KJV

Let us then . . . boldly draw near to the throne of grace . . .
that we may . . . find grace to help . . . [appropriate help
and well-timed help, coming just when we need it].
Hebrews 4:16 AMP

I'm to trust in You at all times, I and all people.
I am to pour out my heart before You;
You, God, are a refuge for me.
Psalm 62:8 PERSONALIZED

HEAVENLY FATHER,

The gut-wrenching pain is more than I can bear. I ask, "Why has this happened to me?" but the answer doesn't come. "It's so unfair; how could You let my child be taken from me?" I demand, with rage and despair.

When there seem to be no answers, I must rely on Your very nature that does not change. It is the thief who comes to steal, kill, and destroy, not You, my Father. And when I've poured out my heart to You, "You have collected all my tears in your bottle. You have recorded each one in your book" (Psalm 56:8 NLT). You really do care for me.

Although this child was a part of my past, I'm encouraged as You remind me this priceless one is also a part of my future. Though the days seem long and painful here, I have Your assurance that brighter days are ahead when I will never again be separated from the precious child You've given me.

AMEN.

Grief
Loss of a Friend or Loved One

Brothers, we do not want you to be ignorant about those who fall asleep, or to grieve like the rest of men, who have no hope. We believe that Jesus died and rose again and so we believe that God will bring with Jesus those who have fallen asleep in him.
1 Thessalonians 4:13-14 NIV

I will ransom them from the power of the grave;
I will redeem them from death.
O Death, I will be your plagues!
O Grave, I will be your destruction!
Hosea 13:14 NKJV

We are always confident; even though we know that while we are at home in the body we are away from the Lord.
2 Corinthians 5:6 NRSV

The believers who are dead will be the first to rise to meet the Lord. Then we who are still alive and remain on the earth will be caught up with them in the clouds to meet the Lord in the air and remain with him forever. So comfort and encourage each other with this news.
1 Thessalonians 4:16-18 TLB

O death, where is your sting [to harm or distress me]?
O death, where is your victory [over me]?
1 Corinthians 15:55 PERSONALIZED

COMFORTING FATHER,

The death of a close friend or loved one is one of the most difficult things I've encountered. Life is but a vapor and then, suddenly, it is gone; where did the time go? So much more we wanted to do, so many more happy memories left to create. And now it is over, and the sadness of this void breaks my heart.

Death was never part of Your plan, and that is one reason it feels so wrong. Unbroken fellowship and joy is what You had in mind. I am thankful You sent Jesus, so we could have a second chance to live forever with You and the ones we hold so dear. In Christ death holds no victory, and even its sting cannot sink in with the despair of the hopeless.

Although no one can ever take this person's place, I ask You to fill the void with Your comfort and Your love, as I look with hope toward Heaven.

AMEN.

Grief
Over Miscarriage

The death of one that belongs to the LORD
is precious in his sight.
Psalm 116:15 NCV

When I suffer, this comforts me:
Your promise gives me life.
Psalm 119:50 NCV

I am he who will sustain you.
I have made you and I will carry you.
Isaiah 46:4 NIV

First off, you must not carry on over them like people who have
nothing to look forward to, as if the grave were the last word.
Since Jesus died and broke loose from the grave, God will
most certainly bring back to life those who died in Jesus.
1 Thessalonians 4:13-14 THE MESSAGE

*I who am alive and remain shall be caught up together
with them [the dead] in the clouds to meet You in the air,
Lord; and in this way we shall always be with You. In this
way we are to comfort one another with these words.*
1 Thessalonians 4:17-18 PERSONALIZED

HEAVENLY FATHER,

If my child had lived a few years on earth, others would
be more understanding of the agony that I feel. They don't
mean to be insensitive, but they have not walked in my
shoes, and they just don't know. But You know, and that
comforts my broken heart.

You are intimately acquainted with the baby whom You
knit together in my womb. I am consoled, knowing my precious one is with You.

I may not have been able to share this earthly life with
my little one, but knowing this child is part of my future
gives me hope. The days here on earth seem like eternity,
being filled with such pain, but they are fleeting compared
to the unending life we will have with You. Heaven will be
a place of precious reunion for my child and me, and in
that day, no more tears will be shed. Our days will be filled
with rejoicing, and we will never be separated again.

AMEN.

Guidance
Overcoming Confusion

*You will keep on guiding me all my life with your wisdom and
counsel, and afterwards receive me into the glories of heaven!*
Psalm 73:24 TLB

*God is not the author of confusion, but of peace,
as in all churches of the saints.*
1 Corinthians 14:33 KJV

*Trust in the LORD with all your heart,
And lean not on your own understanding;
In all your ways acknowledge Him,
And He shall direct your paths.*
Proverbs 3:5-6 NKJV

*We are destroying speculations and every lofty thing
raised up against the knowledge of God, and we are
taking every thought captive to the obedience of Christ.*
2 Corinthians 10:5 NASB

I'm to let Your peace rule in my heart.
Colossians 3:15 PERSONALIZED

ALL-WISE FATHER,

Sometimes I get so confused that I don't know which way is up. I have so many decisions and choices to make, and some will affect the whole course of my life. Fear then joins the parade as an endless list of questions racks my brain.

Only You know my future, Father, and You have already prepared a path for my feet. As I seek You with my whole heart and commit my works to You, You said my thoughts would be established, and I would know which road to travel.

Ultimately, Your peace is what is to dictate my decisions. Like an umpire who must make the critical calls that often determine the outcome of the game, Your peace settles the questions that arise in my mind. I trust You to keep my feet from falling and to help me arrive at the destination You've ordained.

AMEN.

Guidance
Knowing God's Voice

I will instruct you and teach you in the way which you should go;
I will counsel you with My eye upon you.
Psalm 32:8 NASB

Whether you turn to the right or to the left,
your ears will hear a voice behind you, saying,
"This is the way; walk in it."
Isaiah 30:21 NIV

"When he has brought out all his own, he goes ahead of them,
and the sheep follow him because they know his voice."
John 10:4 NRSV

The LORD will cause His glorious voice to be heard.
Isaiah 30:30 NKJV

I will bless You, LORD, who have given me counsel;
my innermost being also instructs me in the night.
Psalm 16:7 PERSONALIZED

HEAVENLY FATHER,

Jesus said that as one of His sheep, I will know His voice and will follow Him. He assured me that I would recognize His voice and not be misled by other voices. You even said I will hear a word behind me saying, "This is the way, walk in it" (Isaiah 30:21 NKJV), so I will know which way to go.

I know you said one place I can hear Your voice is in Your Word. Please, light my path when darkness tries to obscure my way. Every verse comes from You and is written for my benefit. I will read Your Word, Father, and I will sit in the stillness and listen in my heart for Your Shepherd voice.

Let me grow closer to You and become more intimately acquainted with Your voice.

AMEN.

Guilt from Sin

Keep me from deliberate sins!
Don't let them control me.
Then I will be free of guilt
and innocent of great sin.
Psalm 19:13 NLT

God's kindness leads you toward repentance.
Romans 2:4 NIV

Thou, Lord, art good, and ready to forgive,
And abundant in lovingkindness to all who call upon Thee.
Psalm 86:5 NASB

Lord, if you keep in mind our sins then who can
ever get an answer to his prayers? But you forgive!
What an awesome thing this is!
Psalm 130:3 TLB

*If I confess my sins, You are faithful and just to forgive
my sins, and to cleanse me from all unrighteousness.*
1 John 1:9 PERSONALIZED

MERCIFUL FATHER,

I had good intentions, but I have let You down again. I always mean to do the right thing, but I slip up. I feel tainted from my wrong actions and attitudes. Sometimes my actions are fine, but my motivations are wrong.

I'm so thankful You restore me to that place of oneness with You. The blood Jesus gave is my assurance. All I have to do is acknowledge my shortcomings, and You cleanse me, heart and soul. "Wash me, and I shall be whiter than snow" (Psalm 51:7 NKJV), Your Scripture promises. I'm encouraged. I can leave guilt behind and remember not to condemn myself. Any voice of condemnation I hear in my head on this forgiven sin will not be from You, Lord. And I will not listen. I am forgiven—completely.

Father, with You, I can live unburdened by the past and knowing I am loved and forgiven.

AMEN.

Guilt
False Guilt

In a single victorious stroke of Life, all three—sin, guilt, death—
are gone, the gift of our Master, Jesus Christ. Thank God!
1 Corinthians 15:57 THE MESSAGE

You, being dead in your trespasses and the
uncircumcision of your flesh, He has made alive
together with Him, having forgiven you all trespasses.
Colossians 2:13 NKJV

Having chosen us, he called us to come to him; and when we
came, he declared us "not guilty," filled us with Christ's goodness,
gave us right standing with himself, and promised us his glory.
Romans 8:30 TLB

God declares us "not guilty" of offending him if we trust in
Jesus Christ, who in his kindness freely takes away our sins.
Romans 3:24 TLB

There is therefore now no condemnation
for me; I am in Christ Jesus.
Romans 8:1 PERSONALIZED

HEAVENLY FATHER,

I am a prisoner of guilt and a heavy feeling of unworthiness. If I knew of some wrong I had committed, I'd confess it and move on; but I can't think what I did wrong. I feel stuck, robbed of my joy. I am unable to enjoy Your light and have lost my song of joy.

Thank You that You do not leave me in this condition to fend for myself. No, You encourage me with Your Word and reveal my safe position as Your child. Because Jesus ransomed me, my debt of sin is paid. You help me not to listen to Your enemy, the Accuser, condemning me—even using scriptures! I am forgiven! You beckon me to draw near to You, to come boldly to You. You are not angry at me.

Oh, Father! Am I really safe in Your love? How wonderful!

AMEN.

Guilt
Long-term Regret

As far as the east is from the west,
so far has he removed our transgressions from us.
Psalm 103:12 NIV

I am still not all I should be, but I am focusing
all my energies on this one thing: Forgetting the
past and looking forward to what lies ahead.
Philippians 3:13 NLT

Oh, what joy for those whose disobedience is forgiven,
whose sins are put out of sight.
Yes, what joy for those
whose sin is no longer counted against them by the Lord.
Romans 4:7-8 NLT

What happiness for those whose guilt has been forgiven!
What joys when sins are covered over! What relief for those who
have confessed their sins and God has cleared their record.
Psalm 32:1-2 TLB

*You, even You, are He who blots out my transgressions
for Your own sake, and will not remember my sins.*
Isaiah 43:25 PERSONALIZED

REDEEMING FATHER,

Forgiveness sounds so simple: just confess my sin and receive Your cleansing. But what about those wrongs I have committed that have long-term effects on myself or others? How can I be free when the injury seems to continually repeat itself, with no ending in sight? There are some things that just seem too difficult to forgive, and that is where I feel I am.

Regret is like a cancer, feeding on my guilt and draining the life right out of me. It's like a shadow that follows me wherever I go; no matter where I turn, it is always there, refusing to let me forget.

"I can work it all out for good," You remind me as I turn to face You. And suddenly I know, the key is trusting in You. No matter what I've done or the pain I have caused, You can take the broken pieces and create something beautiful that will glorify You. Thank You, Heavenly Father.

AMEN.

Happiness

You have endowed him with eternal happiness. You have
given him the unquenchable joy of your presence.
Psalm 21:6 TLB

Blessings on all who reverence and trust
the Lord—on all who obey him!
Their reward shall be prosperity and happiness.
Psalm 128:1-2 TLB

Ill-gotten gain brings no lasting happiness; right living does.
Proverbs 10:2 TLB

"Don't be afraid, little flock. For it gives your Father
great happiness to give you the Kingdom."
Luke 12:32 NLT

For You, L<small>ORD</small>, have made me glad through Your work:
I will triumph in the works of Your hands.
Psalm 92:4 P<small>ERSONALIZED</small>

J<small>OYFUL</small> F<small>ATHER</small>,

The whole world is searching for happiness, mostly in all the wrong places. But I've discovered that the more involved I allow You to be in my life, the happier and more at peace I become. Unlike getting a "happiness fix" from entertainment or some other fleeting distraction, You provide a river of life that never runs dry.

I find it is the simplest things that make me happiest—my child's hand in mine, a note of encouragement from a friend, the sound of falling rain, listening to the birds sing at daybreak. Each is treasure from Your heart to mine.

Whether it is recognizing Your hand in a person's life or enjoying the grandeur of Your creation, Your works give me a happy heart. I ask You to forgive me for looking to temporal pleasures to fill the void in my life. Fill me with Your song today.

A<small>MEN</small>.

Health

A joyful heart is good medicine,
But a broken spirit dries up the bones.
Proverbs 17:22 NASB

Do not be wise in your own eyes;
fear the LORD and shun evil.
This will be health to your body
and nourishment to your bones.
Proverbs 3:7-8 NIV

Unto you that fear my name shall
the Sun of righteousness arise
with healing in his wings.
Malachi 4:2 KJV

Are any among you sick? They should call for the elders of
the church and have them pray over them, anointing them
with oil in the name of the Lord. The prayer of faith will
save the sick, and the Lord will raise them up.
James 5:14-15 NRSV

By Your stripes I was healed.
1 Peter 2:24 PERSONALIZED

HEAVENLY FATHER,

Good health is something I have taken for granted until now that I am sick. I ask You to forgive me for not being more appreciative when things were going well. Whether it is a cold or a more serious disease, Jesus provided for my healing just as He did for my forgiveness. What an amazing God You are that You've already taken care of what I need for my spirit, my mind, and also my body.

Jesus revealed how closely forgiveness and healing are associated with one another. He asked, "Which is easier, to say, '*Your* sins are forgiven you,' or to say, 'Arise and walk'?" (Matthew 9:5 NKJV) and then proceeded to heal the paralytic.

Neither one is difficult in Your mind, and I ask You to simplify it in mine. As I meditate on the image of Jesus bearing my sickness as well as my sin, I thank You for the healing I need today and give You praise.

AMEN.

Heartbreak
Personal Heartbreak from Rejection

The LORD will not reject his people;
he will never forsake his inheritance.
Psalm 94:14 NIV

The LORD is close to the brokenhearted.
He saves those whose spirits have been crushed.
Psalm 34:18 NCV

I would no more reject my people than I would
change my laws of night and day, of earth and sky.
Jeremiah 33:25 TLB

"Those who welcome you are welcoming me.
And those who reject you are rejecting me.
And those who reject me are rejecting God who sent me."
Luke 10:16 TLB

You heal the broken in heart, including me,
and bind up their wounds, even mine.
Psalm 147:3 PERSONALIZED

HEAVENLY FATHER,

I hurt! I know everyone gets rejected at one time or another, but that doesn't lessen the heartbreak I feel now. It makes me feel small—that I don't matter. I think, *If only I were this* or *If only I were that then they'd think I was really wonderful and worthy of their acceptance.*

But I know this is a fallacy, for only You can love me in the way I need it most. I never have to perform to earn Your love, and You will never break my heart.

Savior, You know exactly how I feel, for You were rejected on a much larger scale. "A man of sorrows and acquainted with grief" (Isaiah 53:3 NKJV), You actually bore my grief and carried my sorrows away. You are moved with compassion toward me and offer healing for my soul. I pray that You will comfort me as You bind up my wounds and heal my broken heart.

AMEN.

Heartbreak
Over Children

I will heal their backsliding,
I will love them freely.
Hosea 14:4 NKJV

God's gifts and his call can never be withdrawn.
Romans 11:29 NLT

Faithful is He who calls you, and He also will bring it to pass.
1 Thessalonians 5:24 NASB

We look not at what can be seen but at
what cannot be seen; for what can be seen is
temporary, but what cannot be seen is eternal.
2 Corinthians 4:18 NRSV

Being confident of this very thing, that You who have begun a good work in me will perform it until the day of Jesus Christ.
Philippians 1:6 PERSONALIZED

HEAVENLY FATHER,

No one could break my heart like this child of mine has done. I had such high expectations and now my hopes have been dashed. Others can't understand why it hurts so much, but they aren't the ones who gave birth to this precious one. I am the one who first observed how perfectly You formed my child, with so much potential for greatness. Such a unique blend of characteristics makes up the complex whole, nothing short of miraculous. But now things have gone wrong.

Poor choices have been made, my guidance trampled under foot. Rebellion has taken hold, and destruction is ongoing. When will it ever stop?

Your Word gives me hope. Not only did You *begin* a good work in my child, You promise to *complete* that work, no matter how long it takes. I ask You to forgive me for the mistakes I have made that might be contributing to this situation, and I ask for Your mercy to make things right.

AMEN.

Hope

If we hope for what we do not see,
with perseverance we wait eagerly for it.
Romans 8:25 NASB

Everything that was written in the past was written
to teach us, so that through endurance and the
encouragement of the Scriptures we might have hope.
Romans 15:4 NIV

Let us hold fast to the confession of our hope
without wavering, for he who promised is faithful.
Hebrews 10:23 NRSV

You are my hope, O Lord GOD;
You are my trust from my youth.
By You I have been upheld from birth;
You are He who took me out of my mother's womb.
My praise shall be continually of You.
Psalm 71:5-6 NKJV

The hope of the righteous shall be gladness.
Proverbs 10:28

*Now may You, the God of hope, fill me with all joy
and peace in believing, that I may abound in hope,
through the power of the Holy Spirit.*
Romans 15:13 PERSONALIZED

GOD OF HOPE,

Like a lighthouse lifts the spirits of storm-weary sailors,
the hope that You give causes me to look up with confident expectation. Even though the ship hasn't reached the
port yet, the sailors sigh with relief as they know the shore
is somewhere near. I'm in my own storm now, circumstances swirling all around me, but I have hope as I look to
You. Jesus is the light of the world, and He is my beacon
of hope.

No matter how bad things look or if my heart is overwhelmed, You promise to set my feet upon solid ground.
By the power of the Holy Spirit, whom You sent to live
inside me, I abound in hope once more, trusting You will
take me through this hard time. Fill me with Your joy and
peace as I depend on You. I sense my strength growing
stronger as I trust You to see me through.

AMEN.

Infertility

Delight yourself in the LORD;
And He will give you the desires of your heart.
Commit your way to the LORD,
Trust also in Him, and He will do it.
Psalm 37:4-5 NASB

In bitterness of soul Hannah wept much and prayed to
the LORD. And she made a vow, saying, "O LORD Almighty,
if you will only look upon your servant's misery and
remember me, and not forget your servant but give her a son,
then I will give him to the LORD for all the days of his life."
1 Samuel 1:10-11 NIV

"I say to you, whatever things you ask when you pray,
believe that you receive them, and you will have them."
Mark 11:24 NKJV

God blessed them and said, "Have many children and
grow in number. Fill the earth and be its master."
Genesis 1:28 NCV

You make the barren woman to keep house and, even me,
to be a joyful mother of children. Praise ye the LORD.
Psalm 113:9 PERSONALIZED

HEAVENLY FATHER,

I am in deep anguish, crying bitterly as I pray to You. No yearning I have ever experienced compares to this longing I have to bear a child. Isn't this one of the main reasons You created me with the anatomy to conceive and bring forth? Yet things aren't working, and I don't know why.

By including Hannah in Your Word, I see that You have compassion on my condition. She, too, was unable to bear children and grieved as I grieve now. You did not forsake her. As she sought You, You granted her desire. You give me hope, for You are a God of miracles.

And yet I remember also that Jesus had no children, and You said that the one who is barren will have more children than the one who is married. (See Isaiah 54:1.) Father, I lay myself at Your feet. Make of my life what You have planned; and I pray that, like Jesus, You would also give me fruitfulness according to Your will and joy in it.

AMEN.

Injustice

"Will not God bring about justice for his chosen ones, who cry
out to him day and night? Will he keep putting them off?
I tell you, he will see that they get justice, and quickly."
Luke 18:7-8 NIV

When I cry out to You,
Then my enemies will turn back;
This I know, because God is for me.
Psalm 56:9 NKJV

Who would dare tangle with God by messing with one of God's
chosen? Who would dare even to point a finger? The One
who died for us—who was raised to life for us!—is in the
presence of God at this very moment sticking up for us.
Romans 8:33-34 THE MESSAGE

What credit is there if, when you sin and are harshly treated, you
endure it with patience? But if when you do what is right and
suffer for it you patiently endure it, this finds favor with God.
1 Peter 2:20 NASB

Judge me, O LORD my God, according to Your
righteousness; and let them not rejoice over me.
Psalm 35:24 PERSONALIZED

WISE AND JUST FATHER,

I have such a strong sense of right and wrong, and I
know You desire for me to conduct my affairs with justice.
But now I find that I'm the victim of a terrible injustice,
and I need Your help. To speak out and say anything might
sound like I'm being defensive. I want to operate from a
place of strength, instead, and I ask You to show me how.

Jesus suffered the greatest injustice of all when He was
crucified without cause, so He knows just how I feel.
Please comfort me.

And please come to my aid and vindicate me. Surround
me, O Lord, protect me from my enemies. "No weapon
formed against you shall prosper" (Isaiah 54:17 NKJV), You
remind me. You do not mean me to remain a victim. I rest
in You.

Give me wisdom to know what, if anything, I need to do to
turn this situation around. Thank You for seeing me through.

AMEN.

Integrity

The LORD will put a curse on the evil person's house.
But he will bless the home of people who do what is right.
Proverbs 3:33 NCV

Christ, who suffered for you, is your example.
Follow in his steps. He never sinned,
and he never deceived anyone.
1 Peter 2:21-22 NLT

I know also, my God, that You test the heart
and have pleasure in uprightness.
1 Chronicles 29:17 NKJV

Guard my soul and deliver me;
Do not let me be ashamed, for I take refuge in Thee.
Let integrity and uprightness preserve me,
For I wait for Thee.
Psalm 25:20-21 NASB

I'm to be a just woman who walks in her integrity;
my children are blessed after me.
Proverbs 20:7 PERSONALIZED

HEAVENLY FATHER,

Integrity is an attribute I hold dear to my heart. I appreciate when others are honest with me, and it is a way of life to which I am committed. Now I discover that You even bless my children when I walk in integrity. Thank you for the long list of blessings for the honest.

- You show integrity to me. (See Psalm 18:25 NLT).
- You protect me. (See Proverbs 2:7 NLT).
- You delight in me. (See Proverbs 11:20 NLT).
- You give me good things. (See Proverbs 28:10 NLT).
- You guide me. (See Proverbs 11:5 TLB).
- You defend me. (See Proverbs 12:13 TLB).

Give me courage to maintain my habit of doing what is right and speaking the truth even under pressure. When others resent my right and loving actions, please protect me. Let the right thing to do be my guide when I'm uncertain what to do. And, Father, let me be Your candle to light the darkness around me.

AMEN.

Isolation

PRAISE ye the LORD.
I will praise the LORD with my whole heart,
in the assembly of the upright, and in the congregation.
Psalm 111:1

They returned to Jerusalem with great joy, and
were continually in the temple, praising God.
Luke 24:52-53 NASB

Blessed are those who dwell in your house;
they are ever praising you.
Psalm 84:4 NIV

You should not stay away from the church meetings, as
some are doing. But you should meet together and encourage
each other. Do this even more as you see the Day coming.
Hebrews 10:25 NCV

Come, and let us go up to the mountain of the LORD, and to the house of the God of Jacob; and he will teach us, me and other believers, of his ways, and we will walk in his paths.
Micah 4:2 PERSONALIZED

HEAVENLY FATHER,

The stress I am living under is almost too much to bear. My life is spinning out of control, making me want to run away and hide.

While getting away for a break can be a good thing, isolating myself from the body of believers would be a dangerous move. It is the enemy who wants me to go off on my own. Like sheep who have wandered away from the fold, I become open to attack when I'm outside the protection other believers can give me.

You've designed the body of believers to be a safe haven for one another; show me one to whom I can reach out for support. Help me to take advantage of the times of corporate worship so that I can be refreshed by Your presence, and show me what I can change to alleviate some of my stress.

Thank You for the safeguards You've given me to keep me safe.

AMEN.

Jealousy

Jealousy is more dangerous and cruel than anger.
Proverbs 27:4 TLB

Do not let your heart envy sinners,
But be zealous for the fear of the LORD all day;
For surely there is a hereafter,
And your hope will not be cut off.
Proverbs 23:17-18 NKJV

Peace of mind means a healthy body.
But jealousy will rot your bones.
Proverbs 14:30 NCV

Let us behave properly as in the day, . . . not in strife
and jealousy. But put on the Lord Jesus Christ, and
make no provision for the flesh in regard to its lusts.
Romans 13:13-14 NASB

For I dare not . . . compare myself with some that commend themselves; but they measuring themselves by themseves, and comparing themselves among themselves, are not wise.
2 Corinthians 10:12 PERSONALIZED

LOVING FATHER,

If envy is the green-eyed monster, then jealousy is its evil sibling. Neither is flattering, and both try to rob me of my joy. You warn me that "human eyes are never satisfied" (Proverbs 27:20 NRSV), and I confess I've fallen prey to this disease of the soul.

Why am I tempted to compare myself with others? Do I not trust that You will bless me as well? I guess I'm like Peter. As long as my eyes are on Jesus, I'm content and at peace; however, as soon as I shift my gaze to others and compare myself with them, the waves of jealousy and envy threaten to pull me under.

I ask You to forgive me for allowing this attitude to take root in my heart. I want to rejoice with those You bless. Help me to remember to keep my eyes on You and to remember that You do not play favorites. I can put my trust in You.

AMEN.

Joy
Fruit of the Spirit

The joy of the LORD is your strength.
Nehemiah 8:10 NIV

Weeping may linger for the night,
but joy comes with the morning.
Psalm 30:5 NRSV

Be glad in the LORD and rejoice, you righteous;
And shout for joy, all you upright in heart!
Psalm 32:11 NKJV

Blessed are the people who know the joyful sound!
They walk, O LORD, in the light of Your countenance.
Psalm 89:15 NKJV

You will show me the path of life; in Your presence is fullness of joy; at Your right hand there are pleasures forevermore.
Psalm 16:11 PERSONALIZED

JOYFUL FATHER,

Your kingdom is not eating and drinking, but "righteousness and peace and joy in the Holy Spirit" (Romans 14:17 NKJV). What a blessing it is that You want Your children to be glad! Joy is a result of abiding in You, and it provides a secret weapon against the enemy of my soul. When depression tries to pull me under with its heaviness and gloom, joy provides the buoyancy I need to stay afloat.

Joy is also like a well of water springing up within my soul. When the circumstances of life try to scorch me like the sun, I can draw on Your joy to provide refreshment to quench my thirst. As simple as biting into a luscious piece of fruit, I can partake of Your joy in all its fullness by getting into Your presence.

Show me ways today, Lord, that I can draw near to You and experience You as my pure joy.

AMEN.

Joy
Laughter

When Jehovah brought back his exiles to Jerusalem,
it was like a dream! How we laughed and
sang for joy. And the other nations said,
"What amazing things the Lord has done for them."
Psalm 126:1-2 TLB

"Blessed are you who weep now,
For you shall laugh."
Luke 6:21 NKJV

I'm whistling, laughing, and jumping for joy;
I'm singing your song, High God.
Psalm 9:2 THE MESSAGE

When the righteous see God in action
they'll laugh, they'll sing,
they'll laugh and sing for joy.
Psalm 68:3 THE MESSAGE

I who am of a merry heart have a continual feast.
Proverbs 15:15 PERSONALIZED

HEAVENLY FATHER,

Some portray piety as a lifestyle of continual seriousness, but that is not what You have in mind. You enjoy relationships with Your children, complete with all the shades of emotion. To be soberly-minded is necessary at times, but so are times of laughter and mirth. Laughing together and crying together are hallmarks of any intimate friendship.

You want me to become like a little child, and children laugh a lot. Merriment does me good like a medicine, and I need a daily dose. Like a rainbow bursting forth after a dark thunderstorm, laughter acts as a catapult to thrust me out of a negative mindset. This joy is the feast You spread before me in the presence of my enemies, delighting me while they look on in dismay.

Help me to see the humor in the circumstances that confront me today. Help me look on the bright side and to laugh a little, knowing You are working in my midst. Give me Your laughter, Father.

AMEN.

Loneliness

You are complete in Him, who is the
head of all principality and power.
Colossians 2:10 NKJV

You will call, and the LORD will answer;
you will cry for help, and he will say: Here am I.
Isaiah 58:9 NIV

Draw nigh to God, and he will draw nigh to you.
James 4:8

Can a woman forget her nursing child,
And not have compassion on the son of her womb?
Surely they may forget,
Yet I will not forget you.
Isaiah 49:15 NKJV

Behold, You stand at the door, and knock: if I hear
Your voice, and open the door, You will come in
to me, and will sup with me, and I with You.
Revelation 3:20 PERSONALIZED

UNDERSTANDING FATHER,

I'm lonely today. Like a raft adrift on the ocean, I feel like I'm cut off from emotional contact. It can be a blessing to be alone, but this loneliness feels like a curse. What do people do who don't know You? I could turn to fleshly vices to fill the empty void, but they only provide temporary relief and don't really satisfy.

Even though I *feel* alone, I know I am not. Jesus is standing at the door of my heart, knocking, waiting for me to answer. So, Father, I will invite my faithful Friend in. He's always good company and provides a listening ear. And He has promised never to leave.

I am amazed as I realize that You are jealous for my companionship and loyalty. You yearn for me to come to You. Maybe this loneliness is not such a curse after all. It encourages me to seek You. Today I'll take some time to be with You, and put this loneliness to flight.

AMEN.

Longing

Because I have lived right, I will see your face.
When I wake up, I will see your likeness and be satisfied.
Psalm 17:15 NCV

At last I shall be fully satisfied; I will praise you with great joy.
Psalm 63:5 TLB

O GOD, thou art my God; early will I seek thee:
my soul thirsteth for thee, my flesh longeth for thee
in a dry and thirsty land, where no water is.
Psalm 63:1 KJV

Thou dost open Thy hand,
And dost satisfy the desire of every living thing.
Psalm 145:16 NASB

For You satisfy my longing soul,
and fill my hungry soul with goodness.
Psalm 107:9 PERSONALIZED

COMFORTING FATHER,

This longing in my soul is a ravenous hunger, demanding to be filled. Like the ebb and flow of the ocean tide, the yearning eases for a while but faithfully returns again.

I've tried to fill this space with a number of different things. Although many of them are good, blessings from Your hand, none of them quite fits the unique shape that is in my heart. Fleshly vices don't even come close; their end produces death. And they leave me unsatisfied.

I realize You are the only One who can fill this hole inside. This emptiness is a place that You created, where only You can fit. As I seek You with all my heart and give You first place, the other blessings You've given me will take on new meaning. They will begin to fit like the spokes on a bicycle wheel. You are the hub from which all other good things radiate.

Come to me, O Father. I take comfort knowing You will satisfy this longing, filling my soul with Your goodness.

AMEN.

Love
Intimacy with My Mate

Let your wife be a fountain of blessing for you.
Rejoice in the wife of your youth.
Proverbs 5:18 NLT

A man shall leave his father and mother and be joined
to his wife, and they shall become one flesh.
Genesis 2:24 NKJV

As an apple tree among the trees of the wood,
so is my beloved among young men.
Song of Solomon 2:3 NRSV

My lover is mine and I am his.
Song of Solomon 2:16 NIV

Let my breasts satisfy you, my husband, at all times;
and may you be ravished always with my love.
Proverbs 5:19 PERSONALIZED

HEAVENLY FATHER,

I want to love my husband in a way that no other woman could. You've given us the blessing of intimate love, which we share with no one else. It provides the spice, when our marriage becomes dull. It satisfies our physical desires and refreshes us when we become weary. As we come and go with our busy lives, help us not to be like two ships passing in the night. Instead, help us to come back together to provide a place, a refuge, for one another.

Help me to never take this part of our relationship for granted, and show us ways to keep things fresh. When we have challenges, help us to work things out, so we can bless one another in the way You designed.

"*He who* finds a wife finds a good *thing*," (Proverbs 18:22 NKJV). Help me to be the best thing that ever happened to my husband.

AMEN.

Love
Loving My Mate

Houses and riches are an inheritance from fathers,
But a prudent wife is from the LORD.
Proverbs 19:14 NKJV

An excellent wife is the crown of her husband.
Proverbs 12:4 NKJV

Wives, be subject (be submissive and adapt yourselves)
to your own husbands as [a service] to the Lord.
Ephesians 5:22 AMP

If two lie together, they keep warm; but how can one keep
warm alone? And though one might prevail against another,
two will withstand one. A threefold cord is not quickly broken.
Ecclesiastes 4:11-12 NRSV

Nevertheless let . . . me see that I reverence my husband.
Ephesians 5:33 PERSONALIZED

HEAVENLY FATHER,

You tell my husband to "rejoice with the wife of [his] youth" (Proverbs 5:18 NKJV), and I want to give my husband something to be happy about. He is Your gift to me, and I want to be that special blessing to him that You've designed me to be.

My husband is not perfect; neither am I. Nevertheless, You desire me to show respect for him and to be his chief cheerleader. It's sometimes hard, especially when I am hurt, so I'm asking for Your help. Instead of reacting in anger, help me to respond to him in a respectful manner, even when we disagree. And when he fails, he needs me more than ever. Help me to remind him of his strengths and say the right thing at the right time to help him on his way.

Only You can love my husband perfectly, so please fill me to overflowing. Help me to be his better half and to bless him all his days.

AMEN.

Love
Loving Others

This is how we know what real love is: Jesus gave his life for us. So we should give our lives for our brothers.
1 John 3:16 NCV

"A new commandment I give to you, that you love one another, even as I have loved you, that you also love one another. By this all men will know that you are My disciples, if you have love for one another."
John 13:34-35 NASB

"Love your enemies, bless those who curse you, do good to those who hate you, and pray for those who spitefully use you and persecute you."
Matthew 5:44 NKJV

"If you are nice only to your friends, then you are no better than other people. Even people without God are nice to their friends."
Matthew 5:47 NCV

Love suffers long, and is kind; love does not envy; love does not advertise itself, is not conceited, does not behave itself rudely, seeks not her own, is not easily provoked, thinks no evil; rejoices not in wrong, but rejoices in the truth; bears all things, believes all things, hopes all things, endures all things. Love never fails.

1 Corinthians 13:4-8 PERSONALIZED

LOVING FATHER,

Loving Your way is a very tall order; yet, if this is Your standard, I know You've also made a way for me to fulfill it. It's easy to love those who love me, yet there are many who I find difficult to love. I need help.

Before I had my children, it never occurred to me that I would have to "walk in love" toward them. I thought the love would always be there, no matter what they did. That's true on one level; but when they go through difficult phases and challenge me at every turn, it wears me out, and I tend to harbor a grudge. You told me not to even let the sun go down on my anger; I can only do this if You help me.

The truth is, You *are* love, and You live in my heart. Help me to yield to You, then, and to be a vessel of Your love to others.

AMEN.

Mothering
Small Children

Train a child how to live the right way.
Then even when he is old, he will still live that way.
Proverbs 22:6 NCV

She speaks with wisdom,
and faithful instruction is on her tongue.
Proverbs 31:26 NIV

Teach them the statutes and the laws, and make
known to them the way in which they are
to walk, and the work they are to do.
Exodus 18:20 NASB

Recite them to your children and talk about them
when you are at home and when you are away,
when you lie down and when you rise.
Deuteronomy 6:7 NRSV

*You shall feed Your flock like a shepherd: You shall gather the
lambs with Your arm, and carry them close to Your chest,
and shall gently lead those, like me, who are with young.*
Isaiah 40:11 PERSONALIZED

HEAVENLY FATHER,

Raising small children is a task unlike any other I have
faced. It is all hands on deck, 24/7, with very few breaks.
There are few *thank-yous*, little appreciation for the self-sac-
rifice the assignment requires. And yet, sometimes it's the
most rewarding job on earth.

I'm thankful that You gently lead me during this season
of my life. I put even more demands on myself than You
put on me. Help me to relax a bit and to keep my priorities
straight. A spotless house is not that important when my
children need my full attention. Help me to turn a blind
eye to the dust that stands in all the corners.

I know it won't always be this difficult, although new
challenges will arise. Help me to enjoy the special moments
today, each one of them a seed for a precious memory. Give
me strength and enable me to be the mother my little children need.

AMEN.

Mothering
Teens

Wise discipline imparts wisdom;
spoiled adolescents embarrass their parents.
Proverbs 29:15 THE MESSAGE

Three things amaze me,
no, four things I'll never understand—
how an eagle flies so high in the sky,
how a snake glides over a rock,
how a ship navigates the ocean,
why adolescents act the way they do.
Proverbs 30:18-19 THE MESSAGE

Parents, don't come down too hard on
your children or you'll crush their spirits.
Colossians 3:21 THE MESSAGE

When his parents saw him, they were astonished. His mother
said to him, "Son, why have you treated us like this?
Your father and I have been anxiously searching for you."
Luke 2:48 NIV

I'm not to provoke my children to wrath; but I'm to bring them up in Your nurture and admonition, Lord.
Ephesians 6:4 PERSONALIZED

WISE FATHER,

Jesus was a teen once, so You must know what I am going through. So much vitality and optimism; they think they can conquer the world. Other days, raging hormones push them to the other end of the spectrum, driving me to prayer on my knees!

Thank You for the precious teens You have given me. The thrill of youth brings our home to life when they walk through the door. It reminds me of my own youth, such an exciting time of life.

But my teens are no longer small children, and I have to adapt to this new level in parenting. If I hover over them too much, they are sure to draw back. But if I give them too much freedom, they are likely to get hurt. Lord, I need You to show me the middle ground. Give me the wisdom to know where I can ease up their restrictions, but keep me sensitive, so I will know when they need me to step in.

AMEN.

Mothering
Adult Children

Do not do wrong to a person to pay him back for doing wrong to you. Or do not insult someone to pay him back for insulting you. But ask God to bless that person.
1 Peter 3:9 NCV

Show respect for everyone.
1 Peter 2:17 TLB

I prayed for this child, and the LORD has granted me what I asked of him. So now I give him to the LORD. For his whole life he will be given over to the LORD.
1 Samuel 1:27-28 NIV

Do not nag your children. If you are too hard to please, they may want to stop trying.
Colossians 3:21 NCV

With all humility and gentleness, with patience,
I am to forbear others in love.
Ephesians 4:2 PERSONALIZED

HEAVENLY FATHER,

When I gave birth to my children, it was hard to imagine they would ever become adults; yet the time has come, and they are no longer living under my roof. Although I'm still their mother, my role has changed and I need Your help.

It is no longer my job to tell them what they should do. I had eighteen years to invest my values in them, but now they must stand on their own. I pray You will help them and catch them if they fall. At those times when I don't approve, help me to show them the respect they deserve. Whenever possible, I will be quick to extend my blessing.

Help me to keep my tongue and not offer unsolicited advice. Should they marry, help me to accept their spouses as wonderful additions to our family. And if they have children, help me to be the support they need without interfering.

Thank You for helping me adapt.

AMEN.

Motives

"When you do a charitable deed, do not let your left
hand know what your right hand is doing, that your
charitable deed may be in secret; and your Father
who sees in secret will Himself reward you openly."
Matthew 6:3-4 NKJV

Acknowledge the God of your father, and serve
him with wholehearted devotion and with a willing
mind, for the LORD searches every heart and
understands every motive behind the thoughts.
1 Chronicles 28:9 NIV

People may be pure in their own eyes,
but the LORD examines their motives.
Proverbs 16:2 NLT

When you ask, you do not receive, because you
ask with wrong motives, that you may spend
what you get on your pleasures.
James 4:3 NIV

Create a clean heart in me, O God; and
renew a right spirit within me.
Psalm 51:10 PERSONALIZED

HEAVENLY FATHER,

It's not so much *what* I do but rather *why* I do it that is so important to You. Even when I'm not aware of my motives myself, you know the thoughts and intentions of my heart. Jesus said that if a man even looks at a woman to lust after her, he has already committed adultery in his heart. Likewise, if I do good deeds or contribute to the poor, it is of no value if I do these things to be seen by others.

Your Word convicts me when I read it. You say it is a "discerner of the thoughts and intents of the heart" (Hebrews 4:12 NKJV). I desire to operate out of a pure heart with Godly motivations. Help me to heed Your Word and listen. Nudge me when I stray from this path, and help me to rely on You. Thank You that I always have your forgiveness.

Purify my heart, Father.

AMEN.

Obeying God

Restore to me again the joy of your salvation,
and make me willing to obey you.
Psalm 51:12 TLB

Obedience is far better than sacrifice. Listening to him is much
better than offering the fat of rams. Rebellion is as bad as the sin
of witchcraft, and stubbornness is as bad as worshiping idols.
1 Samuel 15:22-23 NLT

This is love: that we walk in obedience to his
commands. As you have heard from the beginning,
his command is that you walk in love.
2 John 6 NIV

"Obedience is thicker than blood. The person who obeys my
heavenly Father's will is my brother and sister and mother."
Matthew 12:50 THE MESSAGE

For it is You, God, who work in me both to will
and to do of Your good pleasure.
Philippians 2:13 PERSONALIZED

FAITHFUL FATHER,

As a mother, it is important that my children obey me quickly and with a good attitude. When they comply, it is such a blessing; but when they challenge my directives, it puts a strain on our relationships. It grieves me to realize that as Your child, I'm not much different than my children.

You would rather I obey You than to offer You money or good deeds, and You promise special blessings when I do. When I am willing and obedient, You promise I will eat the good of the land. That's quite an incentive, but I still struggle.

I need Your help, Father. First, help me to hear Your voice clearly, so I know exactly what You are asking of me. Second, at those times when I'm less than willing, I ask You to create in me the power and desire to obey You.

Forgive me for not always being quick to obey, and thank You for helping me in my weakness.

AMEN.

Peaceful Home

*Be cheerful. Keep things in good repair. Keep your spirits up.
Think in harmony. Be agreeable. Do all that, and
the God of love and peace will be with you for sure.*
2 Corinthians 13:11 THE MESSAGE

*The fruit of righteousness is sown
in peace by those who make peace.*
James 3:18 NKJV

*Let us pursue the things which make for
peace and the building up of one another.*
Romans 14:19 NASB

*"Blessed are the peacemakers: for
they shall be called children of God."*
Matthew 5:9

Your people, including me, shall dwell in a peaceable habitation,
and in secure homes, and in quiet resting places.
Isaiah 32:18 PERSONALIZED

GOD OF PEACE,

Peace is a priceless commodity, and I'm thankful You have promised this for our home. Help us to create the kind of atmosphere that each family member needs to find refuge from our lives outside the walls of our dwelling. As each of us faces challenges on the job, at school, with friends, or at sports practice, may we come home to find the secure, quiet resting place You've promised us.

There are times this peace is threatened. When we take out our frustrations and anger on each other or get into heated arguments, we become like adversaries instead of teammates. Help us to be mindful of one another's feelings and find healthy ways of dealing with our negative emotions. Help us to work together instead of against one another, providing support and encouragement when it is needed.

This kind of home is rare in today's world. Use ours to provide a safe haven for others we know. May they find refreshing and hope when they visit, taking the peace with them as they depart.

AMEN.

Persecution

"You're blessed when your commitment to
God provokes persecution. The persecution
drives you even deeper into God's kingdom."
Matthew 5:10 THE MESSAGE

Everyone who wants to live a godly life
in Christ Jesus will be persecuted.
2 Timothy 3:12 NIV

I am well content with . . . insults, . . .with
persecutions, with difficulties, for Christ's sake;
for when I am weak, then I am strong.
2 Corinthians 12:10 NASB

Bless those who persecute you; bless and do not curse them.
Romans 12:14 NRSV

*Blessed am I, when people revile me, and persecute me, and
say all manner of evil against me falsely, for Your sake. I'm to
rejoice, and be exceedingly glad; for great is my reward in heaven:
for so they persecuted the prophets who came before me.*
Matthew 5:11-12 PERSONALIZED

FATHER OF MERCIES,

Being persecuted is tough. Jesus explained it is inevitable,
but when I'm in the line of fire, it's very hard. I don't like
how it feels to be rejected, and it makes me want to draw
back. Standing up for Christ is risky business. The price
can be very high.

But I want to be the kind of believer who is not ashamed
of the Gospel; I want Jesus to be proud of me. Make me
the salt of the earth, never to lose my influence for good. I
want to whet the appetite of unbelievers, creating a hunger
to know You.

Give me courage and boldness not to back down from persecution but to respond in love as Jesus did. As for the price
I may pay, I trust You to work everything out for my good,
knowing there is a great reward waiting for me in Heaven.

AMEN.

Prayer
Interceding for Others

*The Spirit also helps in our weaknesses. For we do not know
what we should pray for as we ought, but the Spirit Himself
makes intercession for us with groanings which cannot be uttered.*
Romans 8:26 NKJV

*He is able to save completely those who come to God
through him, because he always lives to intercede for them.*
Hebrews 7:25 NIV

*He who searches the hearts knows what the mind
of the Spirit is, because He makes intercession
for the saints according to the will of God.*
Romans 8:27 NKJV

*Christ Jesus, who died—more than that, who was raised to life—
is at the right hand of God and is also interceding for us.*
Romans 8:34 NIV

*Supplications, prayers, intercessions, and giving of thanks,
are to be made by me for all people; for kings, and for all
who are in authority; that I may lead a quiet and
peaceable life in all godliness and honesty.*
1 Timothy 2:1-2 PERSONALIZED

FAITHFUL FATHER,

I am privileged to pray on behalf of others, and it is
something You want me to do. Help me to come to You
regularly with requests, not only for my family and friends,
but also for my spiritual and civil leaders. Give our leaders
wisdom, Father. Give our country peace, and give
Christians the freedom to live quietly in Your blessings.

Help me spend some of my prayer time each day listening to You so that I hear what you think about these things
and pray according to Your will to change my world.

Your promises are powerful weapons that I can use in
prayer against the enemy. Bring to my mind in a timely
manner the ones different individuals need. Help me to be
sensitive to Your Spirit as He reveals who needs prayer at a
given moment.

Thank You for this exciting opportunity to be used by You.

AMEN.

Prayer
Conversing with the Father

Come, let's talk this over! says the Lord.
Isaiah 1:18 TLB

The LORD would speak to Moses face to face,
as a man speaks with his friend.
Exodus 33:11 NIV

"Here's what I want you to do: Find a quiet, secluded place so
you won't be tempted to role-play before God. Just be there as
simply and honestly as you can manage. The focus will shift
from you to God, and you will begin to sense his grace."
Matthew 6:6 THE MESSAGE

I think of you on my bed,
and meditate on you in the watches of the night;
for you have been my help. . . .
My soul clings to you.
Psalm 63:6-8 NRSV

Truly my fellowship is with You, Father, and with
Your Son Jesus Christ. . . . that my joy may be full.
1 John 1:3-4 PERSONALIZED

HEAVENLY FATHER,

When I explore the true meaning of prayer, I realize that
in its most basic sense, it is conversing with You. It is not
only what I say to You that counts but what You say to me
as well. No healthy relationship is one-sided, and that
includes the relationship You and I share through prayer.

I appreciate that I can come boldly to You for help when
I need it. Thank You that I can be open and honest with
You and pour out my whole heart to You as David did. You
know the thoughts and motives of my heart anyway, so I
might as well not try to hide my feelings. When I struggle,
it is comforting to know You care and will help me work
things out.

Help me to be a good listener too. I want You to share
Your heart and concerns with me. I want to be Your friend.

AMEN.

Pride

All who fear the LORD will hate evil. That is why I hate pride,
arrogance, corruption, and perverted speech.
Proverbs 8:13 NLT

When pride comes, then comes shame;
But with the humble is wisdom.
Proverbs 11:2 NKJV

Pride ends in a fall, while humility brings honor.
Proverbs 29:23 TLB

The world offers only the lust for physical pleasure,
the lust for everything we see, and pride in our possessions.
These are not from the Father. They are from this evil world.
1 John 2:16 NLT

Pride goes before destruction,
and an arrogant spirit before a fall.
Proverbs 16:18 PERSONALIZED

HEAVENLY FATHER,

Pride takes on many forms, and it is something You despise. To think I am better than another, to not ask for help when I need it, to refuse a gift when it is offered, to not do good when it is within my power—all of these are symptomatic of pride. To think that I could ever earn salvation or any of Your blessings would reveal pride at the root.

I'm thankful You have waved a red flag of caution to alert me because I can slip into pride without even realizing it. And since pride comes before destruction, I want to steer clear of it at all times.

It is good news that I can humble myself when pride rears its ugly head, and in response You promise to lift me up. You will save me and give me grace and wisdom; humility helps me retain honor.

Father, I always want to be Your humble servant, a child who delights Your heart.

AMEN.

Protection

You have made the LORD, my refuge,
Even the Most High, your dwelling place.
No evil will befall you,
Nor will any plague come near your tent.
For He will give His angels charge concerning you,
To guard you in all your ways.
Psalm 91:9-11 NASB

The angel of the LORD encamps all around those who fear Him,
And delivers them.
Psalm 34:7 NKJV

He fills me with strength and protects me wherever I go.
He gives me the surefootedness of a mountain goat upon
the crags. He leads me safely along the top of the cliffs.
Psalm 18:32-33 TLB

God is alive! Praise him who is the great rock of protection.
Psalm 18:46 TLB

*Because I have set my love upon You, Lord,
therefore You will deliver me: You will set me
on high, because I have known Your name.*
Psalm 91:14 PERSONALIZED

FAITHFUL FATHER,

There are so many dangers in the world, and it is not humanly possible to protect myself or my children at all times. I need a supernatural God to do that, and I am thankful You are faithful to guard us. You give Your angels responsibilities to take care of us, and they will deliver us when necessary.

You promise that no plague will come near the dwelling of those who live under Your protection. What an awesome God You are! Help me to trust in You and not put my confidence in unreliable things for safety.

I don't ever want to take Your watchfulness for granted, so today I give You praise for Your constant protection. And I ask that You would protect me and my loved ones from the things I see that threaten our safety today.

AMEN.

Reconciliation
To God

*Now you are no longer strangers to God and foreigners
to heaven, but you are members of God's very own
family, citizens of God's country, and you belong in
God's household with every other Christian.*
Ephesians 2:19 TLB

*If when we were enemies we were reconciled to God
through the death of His Son, much more, having been
reconciled, we shall be saved by His life.*
Romans 5:10 NKJV

*All these things are from God, who reconciled us to Himself
through Christ, and gave us the ministry of reconciliation.*
2 Corinthians 5:18 NASB

*You who were once estranged and hostile in mind, doing evil deeds,
he has now reconciled in his fleshly body through death, so as to
present you holy and blameless and irreproachable before him.*
Colossians 1:21-22 NRSV

*You were in Christ, reconciling the world, including me,
to yourself, not imputing our trespasses to us; and have
committed to us the word of reconciliation.*
2 Corinthians 5:19 PERSONALIZED

FORGIVING FATHER,

To have a rift in my relationship with You, or even with
another person, is a distressing thing. I like all of my relationships to be at peace, and I know this delights Your heart.

It is amazing to realize that even before I was conceived,
You sought to repair the breech that would be between You
and me. Jesus took all my sin, my shame, and any other
thing that would separate me from You and nailed it to His
cross. And because of what He did, I am forever reconciled
to You.

It is a privilege that You have given me the task of
sharing this Good News with others. You said I am Your
ambassador, and I want to be faithful to that call. Give me
opportunities to share this reconciliation with those who
are far from You. Is there someone You'd have me share the
Gospel with today?

AMEN.

Reconciliation
To Others

"When you are offering your gift at the altar, if you remember
that your brother or sister has something against you, leave
your gift there before the altar and go; first be reconciled
to your brother or sister, and then come and offer your gift."
Matthew 5:23-24 NRSV

"A new command I give you: Love one another."
John 13:34 NIV

We, who are many, are one body in Christ,
and individually members one of another.
Romans 12:5 NASB

May the God who gives endurance and encouragement
give you a spirit of unity among yourselves as you follow
Christ Jesus, so that with one heart and mouth you may
glorify the God and Father of our Lord Jesus Christ.
Romans 15:5-6 NIV

If it is possible, as much as it depends upon me,
I am to live peaceably with all people.
Romans 12:18 PERSONALIZED

LOVING FATHER,

You have spread Your love to the world through my heart by the power of Your Holy Spirit living inside of me; therefore, I can be sure I have the power to love and forgive the way that You do. You want us to be one big happy family just like I want harmony for my individual family.

Today there is a division between myself and someone else. I know it grieves You, and it grieves me too. It's like a pebble stuck inside my shoe. I can try to ignore it, but it will be a constant irritant until I stop and take care of it. I may never get all my relationships to the level I'd like, but as much as it depends on me, I'll give it my best effort and depend upon You to change my emotions and produce true love.

Help me to take the initiative in this case to forgive.

AMEN.

Relationships
My Relationship with My Friends

Share each other's troubles and problems,
and so obey our Lord's command.
Galatians 6:2 TLB

Two are better than one, because they have a good reward for
their toil. For if they fall, one will lift up the other; but woe to
one who is alone and falls and does not have another to help.
Ecclesiastes 4:9-10 NRSV

"Greater love has no one than this, than to
lay down one's life for his friends."
John 15:13 NKJV

Admit your faults to one another and pray
for each other so that you may be healed.
James 5:16 TLB

Iron sharpens iron; so I sharpen the countenance of my friend.
Proverbs 27:17 PERSONALIZED

HEAVENLY FATHER,

Friends are some of the best blessings You have given me. A true friend sticks closer than a sister, and that's the kind of friend I want to be. Good friends provide companionship, and they challenge one another to grow. I want my friends and I to be better off and closer to You after having spent time together. The deepest friendships are those I have with fellow believers. We share a common bond in You, and sometimes these friends can seem even closer than my blood relatives.

With my ultrabusy life, it is often difficult to have the kind of time with my friends that I'd like. But, Father, I know that for those relationships to flourish, I must invest time in these individuals. Show me where I can carve out a few minutes for a phone call or take time to go out to lunch. Maybe I could simply put a note in the mail telling my friends how much I value them. Thank You for my friends.

AMEN.

Relationships
My Relationship with
My Aging Parents

*"Honor your father and mother," which is the
first commandment with promise: "that it may be
well with you and you may live long on the earth."*
Ephesians 6:2-3 NKJV

*Listen to your father who begot you,
and do not despise your mother when she is old.*
Proverbs 23:22 NRSV

*If a widow has children or grandchildren, these should
learn first of all to put their religion into practice by caring
for their own family and so repaying their parents
and grandparents, for this is pleasing to God.*
1 Timothy 5:4 NIV

Give honor and respect to all those to whom it is due.
Romans 13:7 TLB

*I shall rise up before the gray head, and honor the face
of the old, and fear my God: You are the LORD.*
Leviticus 19:32 PERSONALIZED

HEAVENLY FATHER,

Regardless of my age, I am never too old to show honor and respect to my parents. The relationships we share are complicated. Not only are we each individuals with our own values and opinions, there is a great deal of water that has passed under the bridge of our lives. Some memories are good, and some are painful; nevertheless, they are still my parents.

I ask You to heal any of the wounds we have caused one another and to help us recall the happy times and be thankful. May forgiveness flow freely between us.

As we are aging, our roles are constantly changing. Help us to gracefully flow together as my parents need me more and more. And since I have children of my own for whom I am responsible, please give me the extra grace I need to care for my parents. I ask that our latter days together be better than all the ones up to this point.

AMEN.

Restoration

The Lord God will visit his people in
kindness and restore their prosperity again.
Zephaniah 2:7 TLB

You will give me greater honor than
before, and turn again and comfort me.
Psalm 71:21 TLB

"The Son of Man came to find and restore the lost."
Luke 19:10 THE MESSAGE

Out of sheer generosity he put us in right standing
with himself. A pure gift. He got us out of the mess we're
in and restored us to where he always wanted us to be.
And he did it by means of Jesus Christ.
Romans 3:24 THE MESSAGE

You will restore to me the years that the locust have eaten. . . .
I shall eat in plenty, and be satisfied, and praise the name
of the LORD my God, who has dealt wondrously
with me; and Your people shall never be ashamed.
Joel 2:25-26 PERSONALIZED

VICTORIOUS FATHER,

Your enemy has ravaged areas of my life. And Father,
some losses come from Your loving discipline as I have
been disobedient to Your commands. The loss is painful,
and I need Your help. I would have despaired, Father, had I
not believed I would receive Your help, but I know that You
are good.

I know my loss is not the end of the story. Jesus stripped
the evil one of all his power, and You have promised to
restore all he has taken. Thank You for even restoring the
years to me as You renew my youth. Not only that, You can
restore my innocence, for You heal my shame. You want me
to eat in plenty and to be satisfied. What a good God You
are! No situation is beyond Your help, so I rely on You. I
will keep my eyes on You, trusting You for restoration.

AMEN.

Salvation
Of My Children

"All your sons will be taught of the LORD;
And the well-being of your sons will be great."
Isaiah 54:13 NASB

A united family may, in God's plan,
result in the children's salvation.
1 Corinthians 7:14 TLB

The prayer of the righteous is powerful and effective.
James 5:16 NRSV

The wages of sin is death, but the gift of
God is eternal life in Christ Jesus our Lord.
Romans 6:23 NKJV

I must believe on the Lord Jesus Christ,
and I will be saved, I and my family.
Acts 16:31 PERSONALIZED

FAITHFUL FATHER,

When I get down to the most basic desires of my heart, the thing I want most is for my children to be saved. I get a glimpse into how You long for each of us to be saved as I yearn for my own children. You don't want even one person to spend eternity without You, and I share Your longing.

I believe on the Lord Jesus Christ, and I claim Your promise to save those in my household. Please let them see the light of the Gospel. I pray that You will open the eyes of their hearts, so they can see their need for the Savior. Thank You that I can know that You love and long over them even more than I do. I will trust in Your goodness and Your father's heart.

I will continue to trust in You. It is reassuring to remember the great price You have paid through Jesus for my children already.

AMEN.

Salvation
Of My Mate

Be an example to the believers in word, in conduct,
in love, in spirit, in faith, in purity.
1 Timothy 4:12 NKJV

Let everyone be quick to listen, slow to speak, slow to anger;
for your anger does not produce God's righteousness.
James 1:19-20 NRSV

Our fight is not against people on earth. We are fighting
against the rulers and authorities and the powers of
this world's darkness. We are fighting against the
spiritual powers of evil in the heavenly world.
Ephesians 6:12 NCV

The earnest (heartfelt, continued) prayer of a righteous man
makes tremendous power available [dynamic in its working].
James 5:16 AMP

I as a wife am to be in subjection to my own husband;
that, if he does not obey the word, he also may without
the word be won by the behavior of his wife; while he
beholds my pure behavior combined with respect.
1 Peter 3:1-2 PERSONALIZED

HEAVENLY FATHER,

It helps to remember that You want my husband to
accept Jesus as his Lord and Savior even more than I do.
You have promised that all of my household will be saved,
and that includes my husband. I can't even imagine what it
would be like to be separated from him for eternity, so I am
depending upon You.

When I get tired of waiting, I am tempted to try to talk
him into receiving Jesus, but this verse instructs me to let
my actions do the talking. Help me to put a guard on my
mouth and only say those things I feel prompted by You to
say. I pray that You will bring other people across his path
to share the Gospel with him and to set Godly examples.

I pray that You will reveal Yourself to my husband in
such a real way that his only response could be to love You
in return.

AMEN.

Salvation
Of Friends and Loved Ones

*"Pray the Lord of the harvest to send out
laborers into His harvest."*
Matthew 9:38 NKJV

*He isn't really being slow about his promised return,
even though it sometimes seems that way. But he is
waiting, for the good reason that he is not willing that any
should perish, and he is giving more time for sinners to repent.*
2 Peter 3:9 TLB

*I pray for you constantly, asking God, the glorious Father of our
Lord Jesus Christ, to give you wisdom to see clearly and really
understand who Christ is and all that he has done for you.*
Ephesians 1:16-17 TLB

*We are therefore Christ's ambassadors, as though God were
making his appeal through us. We implore you on Christ's behalf:
Be reconciled to God. God made him who had no sin to be sin for
us, so that in him we might become the righteousness of God.*
2 Corinthians 5:20-21 NIV

Whoever will call upon the name of the Lord
will be saved, [even my friends or loved ones].
Romans 10:13 PERSONALIZED

HEAVENLY FATHER,

I pray for the salvation of my friends and loved ones who do not know You. You don't want even one person to perish, but You want all of us to come to the knowledge of the truth. I'm so glad, Father, that this includes the people for whom I am praying.

I ask that You would open their spiritual eyes and break the bondage of deception. Send Christians across their paths to share about Your truth, and make me sensitive to know when You want me to share with them. May my life be a shining example of a believer, and may I represent Jesus well.

I ask You to soften the hearts of these for whom I'm interceding. Take away their stony hearts and give them hearts of flesh that hunger for You. I'm so glad You love them even more than I do.

AMEN.

Self-esteem

How precious also are Your thoughts to me, O God! How great is
the sum of them! If I should count them, they would be more in
number than the sand; When I awake, I am still with You.

Psalm 139:17-18 NKJV

Keep me as the apple of your eye;
hide me in the shadow of your wings.

Psalm 17:8 NIV

I have loved you with an everlasting love;
Therefore I have drawn you with lovingkindness.

Jeremiah 31:3 NASB

"Are not two sparrows sold for a penny? Yet not one
of them will fall to the ground apart from your Father.
And even the hairs of your head are all counted. So do not
be afraid; you are of more value than many sparrows."

Matthew 10:29-31 NRSV

*Behold, You have inscribed me upon the palms of
Your hands; my walls are continually before You.*
Isaiah 49:16 PERSONALIZED

LOVING FATHER,

It is amazing to think that You, Creator of the universe,
care so much about me. Your concern for every single one
of us never ends. There's no limit to Your compassion, and
it moves You to action on my behalf.

It is easy for me to feel insignificant when I realize that I
am only one small being out of all that You've created. How
could so great a King have time for me? Yet You say that
You've inscribed me on the palms of Your hands and that
Your thoughts of me are as numerous as the grains of sand.
Continually You think of me, You forgive me, and You
delight in me, beholding my face and meeting my never-
ending needs, simply because You care.

Father, help me to grow in my awareness of just what
this means for me; and then, out of the overflow, may I
extend this great consideration of Yours to others.

AMEN.

Shame

To her it was granted to be arrayed in fine linen, clean and
bright, for the fine linen is the righteous acts of the saints.
Revelation 19:8 NKJV

Christ loved the church and gave himself up for her to make her
holy, cleansing her by the washing with water through the word,
and to present her to himself as a radiant church, without stain
or wrinkle or any other blemish, but holy and blameless.
Ephesians 5:25-27 NIV

I will sprinkle clean water on you, and you will be clean;
I will cleanse you from all your impurities.
Ezekiel 36:25 NIV

"You are already clean because of the word
which I have spoken to you."
John 15:3 NASB

*Instead of my shame I shall have double; and instead of
confusion I shall rejoice in my portion; therefore in my land
I shall possess the double; everlasting joy shall be unto me.*
Isaiah 61:7 PERSONALIZED

HEALING FATHER,

Even after confessing my sin and turning away from the
things I do that are wrong, I feel unclean and bad, like
there is something wrong with me, something beyond
repair. The pain has gone on for so long that I no longer
shed tears; I am numb now, unable to feel.

Sometimes I want to lash out at You, "Why have You let
this happen to me?" But You did nothing wrong to me;
instead the devil has sought to destroy me. You remind me
that You always answer me, and You rescue me. Jesus went
into the grave with my wrongdoing; but He came back, tri-
umphant and alive. He brought me back with Him, forgiven and completely cleansed. My feelings lie to me, and I
ask help in ignoring those lies.

Resurrection and cleansing—Jesus has provided both.
His blood cleanses me of everything vile. You give me
beauty in place of ashes and turn my mourning into joy.
Thank You, my God.

AMEN.

Solitude

Jesus brought them to a garden grove, Gethsemane, and told
them to sit down and wait while he went on ahead to pray.
Matthew 26:36 TLB

In the morning, while it was still very dark, he got up
and went out to a deserted place, and there he prayed.
Mark 1:35 NRSV

Jesus often withdrew to lonely places and prayed.
Luke 5:16 NIV

When Jesus heard what had happened,
he withdrew by boat privately to a solitary place.
Matthew 14:13 NIV

When You had sent the multitudes away,
You went up into a mountain apart to pray
[and you wish me to follow Your example].
Matthew 14:23 PERSONALIZED

HEAVENLY FATHER,

Although being lonely is never a blessing, to be alone can provide precious times of reflection, meditation, and renewal. In fact, times like this are vital to my sense of well-being. The pressures of life make me think I don't have time to stop and reflect, that it would be a waste of valuable time. The unending list of items on my *To Do* list demands my attention.

But Jesus set a beautiful example for me to follow. Often surrounded by throngs of people, many with urgent needs, Jesus knew when He needed a time away to be refreshed by Your Spirit. Daily He poured himself into His disciples, but He knew when to withdraw from them to be filled again by You. Jesus knew how to maintain a proper rhythm to His life, and I want to follow His lead.

Whether that time is spent conversing with You or simply basking in Your presence, I will put time with You at the top of my priority list. Help me to put our time first.

AMEN.

Stress

Outside Pressure

They cry out to the LORD in their trouble,
And He brings them out of their distresses.
He calms the storm,
So that its waves are still.
Then they are glad because they are quiet;
So He guides them to their desired haven.
Psalm 107:28-30 NKJV

From my distress I called upon the LORD;
The LORD answered me and set me in a large place.
Psalm 118:5 NASB

We are pressed on every side by troubles, but not crushed
and broken. We are perplexed because we don't know
why things happen as they do, but we don't give up and quit.
We are hunted down, but God never abandons us. We get
knocked down, but we get up again and keep going.
2 Corinthians 4:8-9 TLB

He brought me out into a spacious place;
he rescued me because he delighted in me.
Psalm 18:19 NIV

You want me to be still, and know that You are God.
Psalm 46:10 PERSONALIZED

HEAVENLY FATHER,

I am under tremendous stress by the demands others are placing on me. My time is no longer my own, and the pressure is rising by the day. If something doesn't change, I will collapse from the weight of it all.

You say to "Meditate within your heart on your bed, and be still" (Psalm 4:4 NKJV). In the stillness I will realize that Jesus is my Good Shepherd who leads me beside still waters, not troubling waters that threaten to overtake me. You are the One to whom I must submit, and You will take care of me.

You know the situations in my life that demand my all, and I ask that You get involved and change things for my good. Give me the courage to say no when I should. Whoever or whatever is sucking the life from me must submit to You, and I hide under the shelter of Your wings as You perfect everything that concerns me.

AMEN.

Stress
From Within

"The seed cast in the weeds represents the ones who hear the
kingdom news but are overwhelmed with worries about all the
things they have to do and all the things they want to get.
The stress strangles what they heard, and nothing comes of it."
Mark 4:18-19 THE MESSAGE

The pressure has built up, like lava beneath the earth.
I'm a volcano ready to blow. I have to speak—I have no choice.
I have to say what's on my heart.
Job 32:19-20 THE MESSAGE

All my insides are on fire, my body is a wreck.
I'm on my last legs; I've had it. . . .
I'm on the edge of losing it—
the pain in my gut keeps burning. . . .
Hurry and help me;
I want some wide-open space in my life!
Psalm 38:7-8,17,22 THE MESSAGE

You will keep in perfect peace all who trust in you,
whose thoughts are fixed on you!
Isaiah 26:3 NLT

*Surely I have behaved and quieted myself, as a child who is
weaned of her mother: my soul is even as a weaned child.*
Psalm 131:2 PERSONALIZED

GOD OF PEACE,

I am under so much pressure that I feel like I could
burst. The demands on my time and energy are never
ending, and my life has become one big "have to." But I add
to the stress by demanding that I do everything perfectly
and that I do more than You are asking me to. This is not
what You want for me. You are the God of Peace, not the
God of Stress. In the midst of my stress, You offer Your
peace as the antidote.

Realistically I cannot continue at the pace I've been
going. If I do not heed Your warnings to slow down, my
body will begin to reflect the wear and tear, and I could
make myself vulnerable to any number of ailments.

Teach me to reevaluate my priorities and only do those
things that are directed by You. Help me to let go of those
things that are not right for me at this time and not to feel
guilty about taking care of myself.

AMEN.

Temptation

Blessed is the man who perseveres under trial, because
when he has stood the test, he will receive the crown
of life that God has promised to those who love him.
James 1:12 NIV

No temptation has overtaken you but such as is common to man;
and God is faithful, who will not allow you be tempted beyond
what you are able, but with the temptation will provide
the way of escape also, so that you may be able to endure it.
1 Corinthians 10:13 NASB

The Lord knows how to deliver the godly out of temptations.
2 Peter 2:9 NKJV

No one, when tempted, should say, "I am being tempted
by God"; for God cannot be tempted by evil and
he himself tempts no one. But one is tempted by
one's own desire, being lured and enticed by it.
James 1:13-14 NRSV

Your word I have hidden in my heart,
so that I might not sin against You.
Psalm 119:11 PERSONALIZED

MY REFUGE,

I don't know what I would do without You. I am being assaulted by temptation right now, and I need Your help. Come to my aid and rescue me.

Thank You for the tools You've given me to overcome temptation. You don't want me to just grit my teeth and bear it; You, yourself, step in to help me. You've given me the Holy Spirit whom I pray will strengthen me with His ability to be righteous inside and out. By hiding Your Word in my heart, the Holy Spirit can bring the appropriate verse to mind, and I can use Your Word as a sword against the enemy as Jesus did. You promised that if I would resist the tempter, he would flee from me.

And if temptation continues to nip at my heels, You promise to provide me a way of escape. I can always run away from temptation and find refuge in You. Thank You for Your help in time of need. Come close, for I need you now.

AMEN.

Thankfulness

Enter into His gates with thanksgiving,
And into His courts with praise.
Be thankful to Him, and bless His name.
Psalm 100:4 NKJV

Oh, how grateful and thankful I am to the
Lord because he is so good. I will sing praise to
the name of the Lord who is above all lords.
Psalm 7:17 TLB

What I want from you is your true thanks; I want your
promises fulfilled. I want you to trust me in your times
of trouble, so I can rescue you, and you can give me glory.
Psalm 50:14-15 TLB

How we thank you, Lord! Your mighty
miracles give proof that you care.
Psalm 75:1 TLB

*Let me come before Your presence with thanksgiving,
and make a joyful noise to You with psalms.*
Psalm 95:2 PERSONALIZED

GRACIOUS FATHER,

There are so many things for which I want to give thanks that I hardly know where to begin. It is easy to take things for granted, but I don't want that said of me.

The cornerstone of all the things for which I am grateful is the gift of Your Son. Thank You for providing the sacrifice needful for the eternal well-being of my family. What a thrill it is to be living in a day when I might witness the return of Jesus. Thank You that I live in a free country and am able to worship You at will. I bless You for the home in which I live, the clothes that adorn my body, and the food to sustain me. May I never take for granted my physical body, so miraculously created to function in just the right way.

Lastly, I am humbled by the beautiful family You ordained for me. May our home be continually filled with Your praise.

AMEN.

Tragedy
In the World

"The mountains may be removed
and the hills may shake,
But My lovingkindness will not be removed from you,
And My covenant of peace will not be shaken,"
Says the LORD who has compassion on you.
Isaiah 54:10 NASB

"I have said this to you, so that in me you may
have peace. In the world you face persecution.
But take courage; I have conquered the world!"
John 16:33 NRSV

I have set the LORD always before me.
Because he is at my right hand, I will not be shaken.
Psalm 16:8 NIV

He rescues you from every trap, and protects you from the fatal
plague. He will shield you with his wings! They will shelter you.
His faithful promises are your armor. Now you don't need to be
afraid of the dark any more, nor fear the dangers of the day; nor
dread the plagues of darkness, nor disasters in the morning.
Psalm 91:3-6 TLB

I may boldly say, The Lord is my helper, and
I will not fear what humans can do to me.
Hebrews 13:6 PERSONALIZED

ALMIGHTY GOD,

The world is a very dangerous place, especially with the dramatic rise in terrorism. Then there are the natural disasters from hurricanes, tornados, earthquakes, volcanic eruptions, fires, and mudslides. If I were to dwell on the possibilities involving any one of these, I would be filled with fear and live with a general sense of uneasiness.

But then I remember that the greater One lives in me. You are God Almighty, the Maker of Heaven and Earth. You promise to protect me from all harm, including terrorism, assault, disease, or natural disaster. All of these have the devil as their source, and Jesus has already conquered him.

Your Word tells me that a thousand may fall at my side and ten thousand at my right hand, but danger shall not come near me or my family. We will only look on with our eyes and see the wicked punished. To give in to fear would be to exalt the devil, so, Father, I trust in You.

AMEN.

Tragedy
In Our Family

"Behold, Satan has demanded permission to sift you like wheat;
but I have prayed for you, that your faith may not fail."
Luke 22:31-32 NASB

The LORD is good,
a refuge in times of trouble.
He cares for those who trust in him.
Nahum 1:7 NIV

When the enemy comes in like a flood,
The Spirit of the LORD will lift up a standard against him.
Isaiah 59:19 NKJV

When you pass through the waters, I will be with you;
and through the rivers, they shall not overwhelm you;
when you walk through fire you shall not be burned,
and the flame shall not consume you.
For I am the LORD your God,
the Holy One of Israel, your Savior.
Isaiah 43:2-3 NRSV

God is my refuge and strength, a very present help in trouble.
Therefore I will not fear, though the earth be removed, and
though the mountains be carried into the midst of the sea.
Psalm 46:1-2 PERSONALIZED

HEAVENLY FATHER,

Our whole world has been turned upside down. We are in dire straights right now, and we have to have Your help or we won't make it. Tragedy has struck our family, and we are devastated. If I were to forget that the devil is the author of tragedy, I would be angry at You. But You are a good God, and You are our help in time of need. We've never needed You like we need You now.

I have more questions than I have answers, especially why this has happened The answer doesn't come, and even if it did, I would still have to put my trust in You. I must rely on the truth that You are a kind, loving God, who does only good for His children.

As we navigate through the fog of this tragedy, I pray that You will guide us safely through. Strengthen me, so I can be a support to the rest of my family and point them to You.

AMEN.

Wisdom

If any of you lacks wisdom, let him ask of God,
who gives to all men generously and
without reproach, and it will be given to him.
James 1:5 NASB

The decrees of the LORD are trustworthy,
making wise the simple.
Psalm 19:7 NLT

Let the wise listen and add to their learning,
and let the discerning get guidance.
Proverbs 1:5 NIV

The fear of the LORD is the beginning of wisdom;
A good understanding have all those who do His commandments.
His praise endures forever.
Psalm 111:10 NKJV

For the LORD gives wisdom; out of his mouth comes knowledge and understanding. He lays up sound wisdom for the righteous.
Proverbs 2:6-7 PERSONALIZED

ALL-WISE FATHER,

Life is pretty complicated for me right now. I have more questions than answers, and I'm filled with confusion. I could go in any number of directions, but I don't know which way is right.

Thankfully I don't have to have all the answers. I just need the answer that You promise to give to me. You said that if I ask for wisdom, You will give it to me liberally, so I'm asking for it now. Thank You for the Bible, for it is filled with Godly wisdom and advice. Please highlight the wisdom I need as I read in Your Word. Help me to see the verses that "have my name on them." Help me also to hear when You speak to my heart through Your Holy Spirit.

Your wisdom makes the complicated things seem simple. And though there are many plans in my mind, I pray for my willingness to accept Your advice even when Your thoughts are different than mine.

AMEN.

Worry

"I say to you, do not be anxious for your life . . . .
Look at the birds of the air, that they do not sow, neither
do they reap, nor gather into barns, and yet your heavenly
Father feeds them. Are you not worth much more than they?"
Matthew 6:25-26 NASB

"When they arrest you and deliver you up, do not worry
beforehand, or premeditate what you will speak.
But whatever is given you in that hour, speak that;
for it is not you who speak, but the Holy Spirit."
Mark 13:11 NKJV

I lay down and slept in peace and woke up safely,
for the Lord was watching over me.
Psalm 3:5 TLB

Don't fret and worry—it only leads to harm.
For the wicked shall be destroyed, but those
who trust the Lord shall be given every blessing.
Psalm 37:8-9 TLB

*I'm to be concerned for nothing; but in everything
by prayer and supplication with thanksgiving let
my requests be made known to You, God.*
Philippians 4:6 PERSONALIZED

WISE FATHER,

The "what ifs" of life seem to be the seeds by which worry tries to produce a harvest in me. I find myself wondering, *What if this happens?* or *If that occurs, what will I do about it?* With so many uncertainties in the world today, the cares of this world threaten to undermine my faith in Your promises.

Thankfully, Your instructions guide me toward a more productive approach. "Give all your worries to him, because he cares for you" (1 Peter 5:7 NCV). Like a father concerned for a troubled child, You invite me to share my concerns with You, offering Your assistance if I will allow You to help.

In response, I take the "what ifs" that confront me now, draining me of strength, and I offer each one to You as a prayer. I gratefully place them at Your feet, and rest in calm assurance that You are working out each detail.

AMEN.

31 Days of Prayer

DAY 1 The Lord's Prayer: Our Father in Heaven

You received the Spirit of adoption
by whom we cry out, "Abba, Father."
Romans 8:15 NKJV

Father, I'm so thankful You are my Father and that You have adopted me into Your family. To think that the God of the universe is *my* Father is almost too great to fathom. And to think that whenever I draw near to You, You draw near to me. You are never too busy to listen to my prayers, my concerns, or my fears. As my Father, You care for me, You comfort me, and You watch over me. Amen.

DAY 2 The Lord's Prayer: Hallowed Be Your Name

O LORD, our Lord, How excellent is Your name in all the earth.
Psalm 8:1 NKJV

Father, I bless and exalt Your holy name and the name of Your Son. *Jesus* is the name above all names, and all power of the enemy must bow to it. When two or three are gathered in that name, He is in our midst, and I am to do everything I do in His name. Jesus gave me the authority to use His name against the enemy, and He promised that whatever I ask in His name, He will do. Praise Your holy name. Amen.

DAY 3 The Lord's Prayer: Your Kingdom Come

"As you go, preach, saying, 'The kingdom of heaven is at hand.'"
Matthew 10:7 NKJV

Heavenly Father, it is exciting to realize that the kingdom of Heaven is at hand. Jesus brought Your kingdom to earth, and now it lives in me. Your kingdom "is not eating and drinking, but righteousness and peace and joy in the Holy Spirit" (Romans 14:17 NKJV). It is not a kingdom in word only but in power. Give me opportunities to bring others to salvation that they, too, may become citizens of Your kingdom. May I always be counted worthy of my citizenship there. Amen.

DAY 4 The Lord's Prayer: Your Will Be Done

Teach me to do Your will, For You are my God.
Psalm 143:10 NKJV

Father God, I don't want to be like the Pharisees who rejected Your will, but like Jesus who chose to do Your will above His own. I am thankful for the Holy Spirit because He makes intercession for me according to Your will. Help me to renew my mind so that I may prove that Your will is good, acceptable, and perfect; and may Your will be done in my life as it is in Heaven. Amen.

DAY 5 The Lord's Prayer: Give Us This Day

*"Your Father knows the things you
have need of before you ask Him."*
Matthew 6:8 NKJV

Heavenly Father, it is very reassuring to realize that You promise to provide for all of my needs. You make sure the tiny sparrows get enough to eat, and I trust You to take care of my needs. Like David, "I have not seen the righteous forsaken, Nor his descendants begging bread" (Psalm 37:25 NKJV). You even know what I need before I ask! How wonderful You are, and I praise You for it. Amen.

DAY 6 The Lord's Prayer: Forgive My Debts As I Forgive

*"If you forgive men their trespasses,
your heavenly Father will also forgive you."*
Matthew 6:14 NKJV

Merciful Father, You are good and Your mercy endures forever. Will You help me to develop that kind of mercy in my life? When others wrong me, I'm tempted to get revenge, but You say to bless those who despitefully use me. I am to show mercy and forgiveness to them, so You can show the same to me. If I were to withhold forgiveness, You would not be able to forgive me. Help me to develop a forgiving heart. Amen.

DAY 7 The Lord's Prayer: Lead Me Not into Temptation

Submit to God. Resist the devil and he will flee from you.
James 4:7 NKJV

Father God, temptation rears its head in many forms, and I need Your help to overcome it. Your Word tells me that if I will submit myself to You, becoming obedient to Your will, then I can resist the devil and he will flee from me. I hide Your Word in my heart to give me the strength to resist temptation. I pray that You will not lead me into temptation but that You would deliver me from evil. Thank You for Your timely help. Amen.

DAY 8 The Lord's Prayer: The Kingdom, the Power, the Glory

"All power in heaven and on earth is given to me. So go and make followers of all people."
Matthew 28:18-19 NCV

Heavenly Father, it is an awesome thing to realize that Jesus has all power and He has commissioned me to go and use that power to bring others to Him. You are Almighty God, and You strengthen me with Your mighty power within my spirit. All the praise, the honor, and the glory belong to You; and I look forward to the day when I can join the angels around Your throne singing, "Holy, holy, holy." Amen.

DAY 9 The Fruit of the Spirit: Love

The love of God has been poured out
in our hearts by the Holy Spirit.
Romans 5:5 NKJV

Loving Father, of all the things You could have said about yourself, You said You *are* love. You didn't say you *have* love, but You *are* love; and You live in me. That means that Your love lives in me. When I am persecuted, used, or treated unfairly, thank You that I have Your love living in me to respond the way Jesus would. Help me to develop all the aspects of Your multi-faceted love. Amen.

DAY 10 The Fruit of the Spirit: Joy

The joy of the LORD is your strength.
Nehemiah 8:10 NKJV

Wonderful Father, because the Holy Spirit lives in me, His fruit abides in me too. I want it to grow in abundance. Traditional thinking would have me believe that to be joyful all the time would be frivolous, but the opposite is true. In the midst of trials, Your joy sustains me. I have a confident expectation that You are working things out for my good. What a joy it is to serve You. Amen.

DAY 11 The Fruit of the Spirit: Peace

The LORD will bless His people with peace.
Psalm 29:11 NKJV

Heavenly Father, peace is a wonderful benefit of knowing You. Because I know You are constantly watching over me, I have no need to be anxious or afraid. You are my Protector from my enemies, my safe Haven, and my Refuge from the storms that would assault my life. This doesn't mean I won't experience scary emotions, but underlying all my feelings is Your peace that passes my understanding. It keeps my heart safe. Amen.

DAY 12 The Fruit of the Spirit: Longsuffering

The LORD is longsuffering and abundant in mercy.
Numbers 14:18 NKJV

Father God, I am so thankful You are patient with me. You don't ever tap Your foot, waiting for me to hurry up and get it right. You bear with me for as long as it takes. Help me to extend this same blessing to the people in my life. When I want to get agitated with my children or others, help me to let Your longsuffering love come to the surface. I want to be as abundant in mercy as You are. Amen.

DAY 13 The Fruit of the Spirit: Kindness

Be kind to one another.
Ephesians 4:32 NKJV

Heavenly Father, it blesses me to realize that You are kind, especially when so many view You as an overbearing judge. No, You are kind. That means that I can be kind, too, since You live in me. Kindness may seem like a small thing, but it makes a big impact on the recipient. As I go about my day, help me to look for opportunities to extend extraordinary kindness to others. May they see Jesus as I am kind to them. Amen.

DAY 14 The Fruit of the Spirit: Goodness

As we have opportunity, let us do good to all, especially
to those who are of the household of faith.
Galatians 6:10 NKJV

Gracious Father, I love that You are good and that Your mercy endures forever. You say this so many times in the Bible that it is obvious You want to make sure I get the message. The Bible says that Your goodness makes me great and Your blessings lead me to repentance. How could I not seek forgiveness when You are so good to me? Why would I ever turn You away or distrust You? You are a good God all the time, and I love You for it. Amen.

DAY 15 The Fruit of the Spirit: Faith

*Without faith it is impossible to please Him, for he
who comes to God must believe that He is, and that
He is a rewarder of those who diligently seek Him.*
Hebrews 11:6 NKJV

Heavenly Father, faith in You is the most basic element
of my spiritual life. If I don't believe that You are, then in
whom or in what could I put my faith? You are the only
One on whom I can totally depend, the only One who
does not change, the only One who answers prayer.
Everything begins and ends with You, and by You all things
exist. I do believe in You, and I praise You for rewarding me
as I diligently seek You. Amen.

DAY 16 The Fruit of the Spirit: Gentleness

A servant of the Lord must not quarrel but be gentle to all.
2 Timothy 2:24 NKJV

God, You are a wonderful Father, knowing exactly when to
be firm with me. But You always do it in such a gentle way
that I am never afraid of You. To be corrected by You is a joy
because Your manner motivates me to want to change. When
You discipline me, You give me hope that I can change, and
You even help me do it. Help me to practice this type of gentleness with my children and the others in my life. Amen.

DAY 17 The Fruit of the Spirit: Self-control

He who is slow to wrath has great understanding,
But he who is impulsive exalts folly.
Proverbs 14:29 NKJV

Heavenly Father, self-control is a quality I need help to develop. With so many stresses in my life, it is often easier to give in to anger or other human urges. Restraint is what I need, and I must walk in the strength supplied by Your Spirit to keep myself in check. Thank You for Your help. Help me to hold my tongue, to think before I speak, and to use restraint. Amen.

DAY 18 The Armor of God: Mighty Weapons

The weapons of our warfare are not carnal but
mighty in God for pulling down strongholds.
2 Corinthians 10:4 NKJV

Almighty Father, there are situations in my life that are beyond human control. I've tried everything in my power to overcome them, but it is obvious that supernatural assistance is needed. I am thankful to know that You have provided weapons that are mighty in You and that I am able to use them to pull down these strongholds. With Your help, nothing is too difficult. Your enemy has no power over me, for he must bow to the name of Jesus. Amen.

DAY 19 The Armor of God: Girding My Loins with Truth

"You shall know the truth, and the truth shall make you free."
John 8:32 NKJV

Heavenly Father, Your truth is a powerful weapon. My mind is a battlefield, and it is the place where the enemy tries to plant lies and sow seeds of doubt. If I believe his lies, he has power in that area of my life. But Your Word is truth, and it has the power to set me free. Please bring to my attention any lies to which I've fallen prey, and help me find a word of Your truth to put in its place. Amen.

DAY 20 The Armor of God: The Breastplate of Righteousness

He made Him who knew no sin to be sin for us,
that we might become the righteousness of God in Him.
2 Corinthians 5:21 NKJV

Loving Father, Your approval means everything to me. When I feel unworthy, the enemy can make me believe that You don't really love me and, therefore, I can't count on You to come through for me. But nothing could be further from the truth. Jesus actually became my sin, so I could become Your righteousness in Him. Knowing I have right standing with You acts as a shield over my heart, protecting me from this lie of Satan. Thank You for the gift of righteousness. Amen.

DAY 21 The Armor of God: Gospel Shoes of Peace

Having been justified by faith, we have peace
with God through our Lord Jesus Christ.
Romans 5:1 NKJV

Father of Peace, before I accepted Jesus as my Lord and
Savior, sin separated me from You; and we were not at
peace with one another. This hurt Your heart even more
than mine, and You provided the remedy. Jesus paid the
price for my sin, so I could be at peace with You. Now it is
my turn to share this Good News with others so that they,
too, can be reconciled to You. Send me to someone who
needs to hear this message today. Amen.

DAY 22 The Armor of God: The Shield of Faith

In every battle you will need faith as your shield
to stop the fiery arrows aimed at you by Satan.
Ephesians 6:16 TLB

Heavenly Father, I have faith in You and Your goodness,
which puts me in right standing with You; but it also takes
faith to quench the enemy's fiery darts. It is important that
I fill my heart and mind with Your Word so that when the
enemy throws a dart of sickness, doubt, fear, or any other
ungodly thing, I can quench that dart with an appropriate
promise. No weapon of Satan can penetrate the shield of
faith. Praise Your holy name. Amen.

DAY 23 The Armor of God: The Helmet of Salvation

The hope of salvation should be our helmet.
1 Thessalonians 5:8 NCV

Father, I am so thankful for Your gift of salvation. It gives me hope to know I will spend eternity with You. While I am on Earth, I am tempted to see things from my earthly perspective, but You want me to put on the helmet of salvation and to see things from Your perspective. When I put the helmet on, I see I am saved from any device of the enemy, for You are greater and You live in me. Praise You! Amen.

DAY 24 The Armor of God: The Sword of the Spirit

The word of God is living and powerful,
and sharper than any two-edged sword.
Hebrews 4:12 NKJV

Father, the only offensive weapon You have given me in Your armor is the sword of the Spirit, which is Your holy Word. With it I can be proactive and pull down enemy strongholds. Your Word is living and powerful, and I can use it to wreak havoc in the realm of the spirit. Your truth defeats all attacks of the enemy, for all natural circumstances must submit to what You say. Thank You for watching over Your Word to make it come true. Amen.

DAY 25 Power over Sin

Sin shall not have dominion over you,
for you are not under law but under grace.
Romans 6:14 NKJV

Righteous Father, it is so exciting to realize that Jesus triumphed over all sin, even mine, defeating it for me. When I accepted Him as my Lord and Savior, I became a new creation in Christ. All of my old nature passed away, and now I have Your nature. When sin tries to rear its ugly head now, I can triumph over it because greater is He who lives in me than he who lives in the world. Thank You for giving me the victory. Amen.

DAY 26 God's Promises

All the promises of God in Him are Yes, and in Him Amen.
2 Corinthians 1:20 NKJV

Heavenly Father, Your Word is more priceless than gold to me, for Your promises are true and You always keep them. Whatever I am facing, You have provided a promise to cover that area, and You say yes to all of them. When I pray according to Your will and Your Word, You promise to hear me and to grant my request. Thank You for Your faithfulness to me. Amen.

DAY 27 Prayer: Thanksgiving

In everything give thanks; for this is the
will of God in Christ Jesus for you.
1 Thessalonians 5:18 NKJV

Gracious Father, an attitude of gratitude is essential if I am to maintain a sense of well-being. You encourage me to look up always and to be thankful in any and all circumstances. I don't have to be thankful *for* all things, for the enemy works to destroy, but even *in* trials, I can still be thankful for my many blessings. I can always thank You for working things out for my good because You are faithful to make that happen. Amen.

DAY 28 Prayer: Intercession

Stay alert and be persistent in your prayers
for all Christians everywhere.
Ephesians 6:18 NLT

Dear Father, I notice that in the apostle Paul's letters, he prayed constantly for those under his spiritual direction. He did not just win people to You and then forget about them, but he continually prayed that they would grow up in Christ and be strengthened inside. Whom do I know who could use a boost from prayer power today? Please use me to intercede for them. Amen.

DAY 29 Prayer: Pray without Ceasing

Pray without ceasing.
1 Thessalonians 5:17 NKJV

Heavenly Father, I see that prayer is to be a way of life for me as a believer. It is good to set aside specific times to pray, but I can also be in a constant attitude of prayer as I go about my daily business. Thank You for giving me the Holy Spirit to help me know what to pray. And since prayer is a two-way communication, help me to listen and enjoy Your company. Amen.

DAY 30 Prayer: Worship

"God is Spirit, and those who worship
Him must worship in spirit and truth."
John 4:24 NKJV

Holy Father, something from deep within me longs to worship You. It is in those times of intimacy that I can see You clearly and get in touch with Your heart. It is during those times that You do deep work in my innermost being, helping me to grow up in Christ. It is a preview of the day when I will worship around Your throne forever. You are so worthy of any praise and adoration I could give You. You are my all in all. Amen.

DAY 31 Giving Thanks for Eternal Life

They need no lamp nor light of the sun, for the Lord God
gives them light. And they shall reign forever and ever.
Revelation 22:5 NKJV

Heavenly Father, the moment I received Jesus into my
heart, my eternal life began. I am now in covenant with You
and will spend eternity in Your presence. Even the best day
here is nothing compared to any day in Heaven; it is so
grand that I cannot conceive of the glory. It is my blessed
hope, and I keep the thought of it before me at all times. I
want to concentrate on doing those things that will matter
into eternity. Each day help me to invest something into my
future with You. Amen.

My Personal Prayer Requests

God's Answers to My Personal Prayers

_____

_____

_____

_____

_____

_____

_____

_____

_____

_____

_____

My Personal Prayer Requests

God's Answers to My Personal Prayers

_____

_____

_____

_____

_____

_____

_____

_____

_____

_____

_____

_____

_____

_____

_____

_____

My Personal Prayer Requests

God's Answers to My Personal Prayers

_____

_____

_____

_____

_____

_____

_____

_____

_____

_____

_____

_____

_____

_____